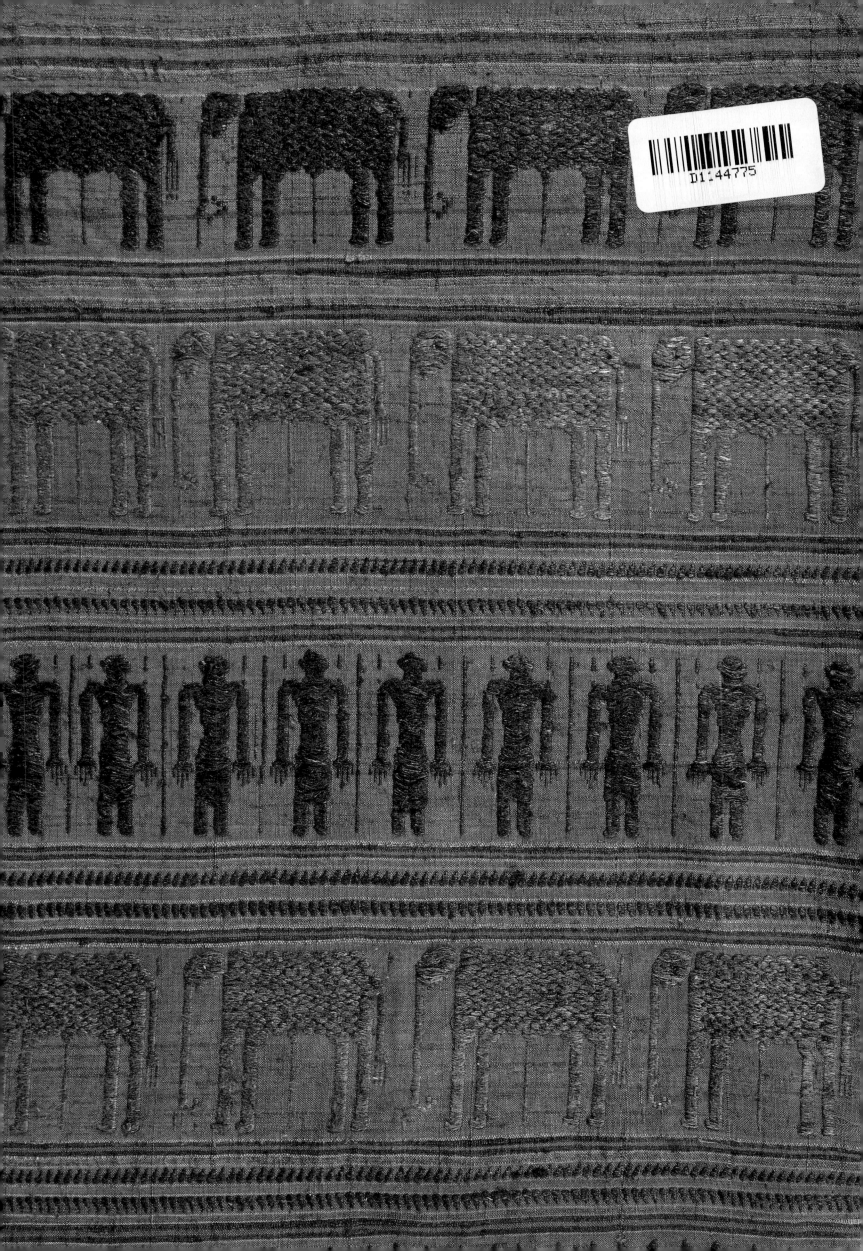

THE ELEPHANT IN THAI LIFE & LEGEND
Copyright © 1998 Monsoon Editions
First Edition 1998
ISBN: 974-86302-9-3
Published by Monsoon Editions Ltd. Partnership,
245/3 Sukhumvit 21, Bangkok 10110, Thailand,
Tel & Fax: (66-2) 258-7184
E-mail: pimpa@loxinfo.co.th
Color separation by S. Film & Plate Co. Ltd.

Gold Sponsors:
National Energy Policy Office (NEPO),
Advance Agro Public Co., Ltd.
Silver Sponsor:
Thai Airways International Public Co., Ltd.

This book is entirely printed on paper from Advance Agro
where paper comes from 100% tree farms, hence
preserving our natural forests.

Cover-jacket photo: Gold elephant, decorated with semi-precious
stones, found at Wat Rajburana in Ayutthaya; this was part
of a treasure placed in the temple by King Boromaracha in 1424
to honor two brothers killed in a duel on elephant back.
(Chao Sam Phraya National Museum, Ayutthaya.)
Back jacket: Thailand's former national flag. Devised by King Rama II,
this represented the kingdom until the flag was changed to its present
form in 1917. (Courtesy of The Smithsonian Institution)
End paper: Hand woven silk banner from Chiang Rai.
(Courtesy of Pornroj Angsanakul)
Right: Detail of colored lacquer scripture cabinet from early
Bangkok period depicting an episode from the Jataka tales.
(Wang Chankasem Museum, Ayutthaya)
Page 4: Detail from temple mural at Wat Phumin
in Nan province.
Pages 6-7: Detail from a mural painting at Wat Suthat, Bangkok,
showing elephants of the mythical Himaphan forest.
Pages 8-9: An 18th century French watercolor rendering
of elephants belonging to the King of Siam.
(Courtesy of Bibliothèque Nationale, Paris)
Page 10: Old photograph showing the ruined stupa of
Wat Chang Lom in Si Satchanalai around 1900.
(Collection of Luca Invernizzi Tettoni)

ISO 14001
CERTIFICATE NO. AJA 97/1088

ADVANCE AGRO
ISO 14001 Paper Manufacturer
Using Plantation Tree

Advance Agro is the first integrated pulp and paper
manufacturer in Southeast Asia to be certified for
ISO 14001 Environmental Management Standards.

The Elephant
in Thai Life & Legend

Main photography by
Ping Amranand

Main text by William Warren

Contributing Writers
Richard Lair
Professor Suthilak Amphanwong
Pongpisit Viseshakul (Ph.D.Cantab.)
Pittaya Homkrailas
Peter Cuasay

MONSOON
EDITIONS

Escuries des Ele[phants]

Chaque Elephant a son escurie particuliere bastie ou de brique ou de bamboux et
il a un baston aubout duquel il y a Comme a un Croc de batelier une pointe a[u]
vont ala Campagne assez loin et reviennent le Soir chargez de grandes herb[es]
des Riies entieres autour deson palais qui ne sont composées que de maisons [...]
Leur fait Cuire d'une sorte de grain Comme des Lentilles on y met du poivre long
qu'on appelle Poivre d'elephant on met ce grain en boules grosses Comme la test[e]

...hants et leur manger.

...urs hommes quy le Seruent, on appelle Cornac Celuy qui gouuerne l'elephant
...e autre Contournée dont jl pique le front de l'elephant les autres hommes,
...ur les Elephants Le Roy de Siam a vne grande quantité d'Elephans on voit
...s elephans et Chacune a vne grande porte Cochere a deux battans on —
...qui est noir et dela longeur dela moitié d'vn doigt et tout Chagriné —
...e enfant qu'on met dans la bouche de l'elephant.

Contents

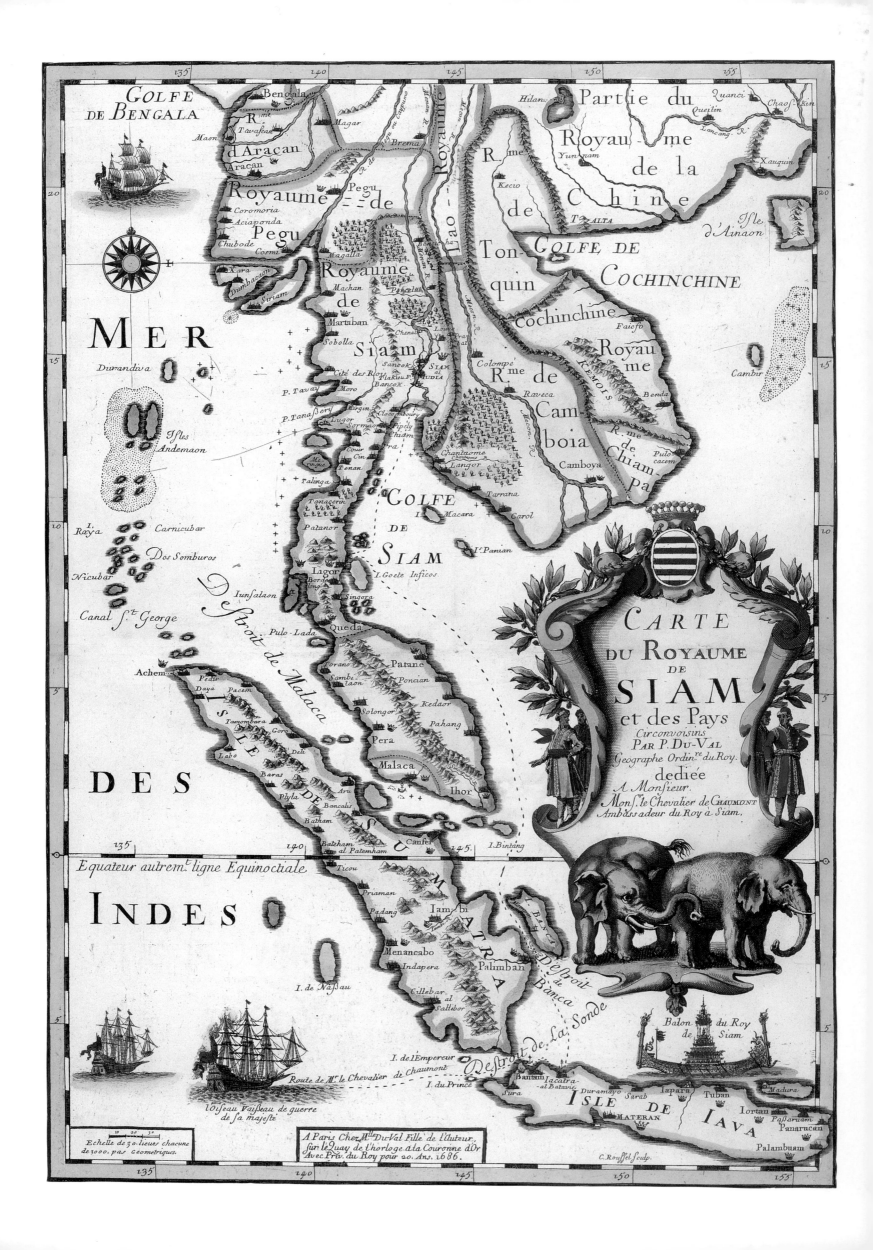

GOLFE DE BENGALA

Bengala
R.me Tavascan
Magar
Maon
d'Aracan
Aracan
Royaume de Pegu
Pegu
Coromoria
Aciaponda
Chubode   Cosmi
Xara
Dumbacan
Siriam
Magalla
Machan
Royaume de Siam
Martuban
Sobolla
Pocelah
Chenak
Cité des Rois
Sancok
Moro
Flakieu R.   SIAM al IUDIA
Bancok
P. Tavay
P. Tanasseri
Virgin   Cloco
Lugor   Amboury
Sormaon   Pipely
Prai   Chiam
Cour   Cin
Tenan
De ringue
Talinga
Tanaserin
Patanor
Lagor Bord long
Iunsalaon
Singora
Pulo-Lada   Queda
Achem
Pedir
Daya   Pacem
Tamombara
Coro
Labo   Deli
Baras
Plyla   Bancalis
Batham
Baleham al Patemham
Ticou
Priaman
Padang   Iambi
Menancabo
Indapera   Palimban
Cillebar al Saltebor
I. de Nassau

MER

Durandiva
Isles Andemaon

DES

INDES

I. Roya   Carnicubar
Dos Somburos
Nicubar
Canal S.t George

D Stroit de Malaca

ISLE DE SUMATRA

Corano
Sambe laon
Solongor
Aru
Canfer

Patane
Poncian
Kedaor
Pahang
Pera
Malaca
Ihor

GOLFE DE SIAM

I. Macara
I. Panian
I. Goete Insicos

Equateur autrem.t ligne Equinoctiale

I. de l'Empereur
Route de M.r le Chevalier de Chaumont
I. du Prince

l'Oiseau Vaisseau de guerre de sa majesté

Partie du Royau-me de la Chine

Hilan
Quanci
Queitin   Chaos-Kin
Lancang. R.
Yun nam
Xauquin
Kecio
T. ALTA
Isle d'Ainaon

Ton-quin
Cochinchine
Faicfo
Royaume
Colompe
R.me de Camboia
Raveca
Chantaome Chanboura
Langor
Camboya
Benda
Pulo cacem
R.me de Chiampa
Tarrana
Carol
Cambir

GOLFE DE COCHINCHINE

Lao   R.me

CARTE DU ROYAUME DE SIAM et des Pays Circonvoisins PAR P. DU-VAL Geographe Ordin.re du Roy. dediée A Monsieur. Mons.r le Chevalier de Chaumont Ambassadeur du Roy à Siam.

Balon du Roy de Siam

I. BANCA
Destroit de Banca
Destroit de La Sonde

Bantam Iacatra -al Batanie
Sura
Duramayo   Sarab
MATERAN
Iapara   Tuban
Madura
Iortau
Passaruam
Panarucan
Palambuam

ISLE DE IAVA

A Paris Chez M.lle Du-Val Fille de l'Auteur, sur le Quay de l'horloge a la Couronne d'Or Avec Priv. du Roy pour 20. Ans. 1686.

Echelle de 30. lieues chacune de 3000. pas Geometriques.

C. Roussel sculp.

Preface

"A mammal of the suborder Elephantoidea, order Proboscidea, characterized by massive size; great strength; a disproportionately large head; long, grasping trunk or proboscis; short neck; thick, loose hairless skin. The name pachyderm, referring to the thick skin, is a holdover from an earlier and now obsolete classification in which the elephants were grouped with such unlikely animals as walruses, tapirs, rhinoceroses, and hippopotamuses under the term Pachydermata."

The language of the *Encyclopedia Britannica* is dispassionate and efficient. It tells you just what an elephant is, from an objective, scientific viewpoint. But it scarcely reflects the wonder, the awe, often the sense of sheer delight that the animal has inspired since the earliest recorded history, that it still inspires in most people wherever they come across it - as star performer in a circus, perhaps, or as part of some festival, thoughtfully viewing visitors at a zoo, or, rarest and best of all, meandering gracefully along a trail in its native habitat. To such observers, the elephant is unique in more than simple vastness; it posesses other, even more distinctive qualities, some of them almost mystical, that set it apart from all other animals and seem to demand a very different sort of response. Especially in Asia, over many centuries, it has played a central role not only in daily life but also in the legends and rituals of half a dozen different cultures.

Of nowhere has this been more true than Thailand. In both physical and legendary form, the elephant has existed as long as the kingdom itself, an intricate part of the culture long before the first written Thai inscriptions were composed. Wild, it roamed the forests in large herds, and elaborate systems envolved for its capture and training. In the service of man, it was long considered almost indispensable - helping to clear the jungles, bearing kings, nobles, and ordinary men on countless journeys, taking part in epic battles; indeed, it was the *cause* of some of the battles. Wealth and power were measured by its possession, especially in one rare form popularly (if not accurately) called the White Elephant which is still to some degree worshipped as a living divinity and for nearly a century symbolized the kingdom on the national flag. Even the shape of the country is frequently compared to that of an elephant's head, with the long southern peninsula serving as the trunk.

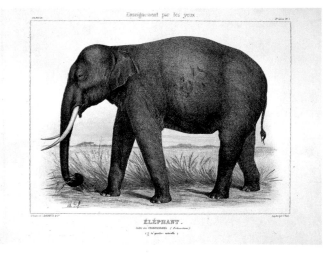

ÉLÉPHANT.

Opposite: Old map of Thailand, a hand-colored copper-engraving printed in Paris, 1686. (Courtesy of the Jim Thompson Foundation)
Above: Lithograph from a children's book printed in Paris, 1860. (Courtesy of Joerg Kohler)

Realistically or imaginatively, the animal appears in every expression of Thai art. Massive, life-like elephants are incorporated into the architecture of ancient temples at Sukhothai and stand guard outside the entrance of the Chakri Maha Prasat Throne Hall within Bangkok's Grand Palace. Fanciful, multi-colored elephants march in processions, occasionally frolic, and sometimes fly through complex mural paintings that adorn temples and palaces or in gold-and-black lacquer decorations, while others are commemorated in the most exquisite mother-of-pearl inlay decorations or rendered by woodcarvers on gilded gables. It is a prominent part of the designs of royal and official emblems, woven into textiles, shaped into ceramics, featured on coins, stamps, cigarette cards, commercial logos, tourist souvenirs, and innumerable other every-day products. Wrote the famous Thai poet Sunthorn Phu in the early nineteenth century, *"I'd like my words, my book,/ To preserve, till the end of time and heaven,/ Sunthorn the scribe who belongs/ to the King of the White Elephant."*

On another level, it has inspired Thai proverbs (such as a famous, controversial one comparing the role of women to the elephant's hind legs and another, less well known, that asserts "When inspecting an elephant, examine its tail; when inspecting your future wife, ex-

amine her mother") and given rise to superstitions (the belief that walking under an elephant brings good luck and, in the case of a pregnant woman, an easy delivery). At the beginning of the 1930s wild Thai elephants were the stars of a spectacular silent movie called "Chang!" directed by Merian Cooper (who later made "King Kong"); toward the end of the same decade a future Prime Minister, Pridi Banomyong, wrote and produced a movie called "The King of the White Elephant," aimed at stimulating pride in the country's cultural heritage.

The elephant also has much to tell us about the kingdom's present. While the conditions that brought it prominence and made it such a vital part of life have changed drastically in recent years, its symbolic role remains as potent as ever. The ceremonial emblem of His Majesty King Bhumibol Adulyadej's Golden Jubilee celebration in 1996 showed two white elephants flanking the seal of the Chakri Dynasty and bearing seven-tiered royal umbrellas on their backs. To commemorate the twentieth anniversary of the establishment of diplomatic relations between Thailand and China, a set of identical, bilingual stamps was issued, showing two groups of wild elephants coming to drink water from the same river. Supplicants at shrines bring elephant figures to improve their luck and

Opposite: Detail from a door panel at Wat Po, Bangkok, decorated with mother-of-pearl inlay and showing a battle scene from the Ramakien.
Above: Bronze guardian elephants in the Grand Palace compound.

perhaps increase their longevity, luxury hotels and business firms place them outside their doors, tourists buy them in a dozen different forms as a souvenir of their visit.

And the physical animal itself also remains - living, as the noted expert Richard Lair puts it, like the Thais themselves "in a perplexing mix of old and new," a focal point in the struggle to preserve traditional culture in a modern environment. The country's wild elephant population is dwindling - current estimates range from 1,000 to 2,000 - but herds still roam in what remains of the once extensive forests. More visibly to the average person, there are at least 3,500 domesticated elephants, most of them in the north and northeast but also many to be seen as far afield as tourist attractions overlooking the sea in Pattaya and Phuket or wandering the crowded streets of Bangkok, where their mahouts come in the hope of earning badly needed funds for their continued support.

The Thai elephant today is thus a symbol of past power and splendor, encountered in one form or another almost everywhere one looks, and, at the same time, an urgent national conundrum, upon the solution of which may depend much more than the animal's mere survival. In the narrow pursuit of material comforts, Thailand's natural resources are being pushed to the limit to supply more energy for the population and more products for the markets. One direct result is the encroachment on our forests, rivers, and the natural habitats of wild animals. The elephant, revered though it might be in symbolic terms, has become a victim of these reckless tendencies, endangered where it still exists in the wild and too often abused as a domesticated animal.

This book examines both aspects: the richness of the elephant's contribution to our cultural life and lore and the very serious problems it now raises for conservationists and ordinary Thais alike.

Opposite: Bathing in the Mun River is a daily ritual for elephants and their mahouts at Ta Klang village in Surin province. *Above:* A Family of domesticated elephants in Surin, where the famous Elephant Roundup takes place annually.

¼₀.

Der asiatische Elephant.
L'Elephant des Indes.

¼₃.

Ein junger afrikanischer Elephant.
Elephant jeune mâle Afrique.

The Asian Elephant

The ancestor of today's elephant was an insignificant, tapir-like little mammal whose remains, some 45 million years old, have been found in Egypt. From this creature more than 300 related species evolved, some of them dwarfs and others enormous; by the time man appeared on earth, all but three had disappeared. One of these, the vast Woolly Mammoth, whose portrait appears in many prehistoric cave paintings, is believed to have made its exit from the scene about 10,000 years ago, possibly due to a period of climatic warming. This left only two, the Asian elephant *(Elephas maximus)* and the African elephant *(Laxodonta africana)*, both of which currently face an uphill struggle in a world increasingly hostile to their survival.

Asian or African, elephants have certain similar characteristics, most of them unusual. They are large, of course - an adult Asian bull can weigh three or four tons and stand ten feet tall at his highest point - yet do not seem cumbersome as they make their way on remarkable feet pads that expand and contract and allow them to negotiate jungle and field, steep hills and marshland. They are strong, capable of pulling heavy teak logs or carrying loads of about 600 pounds. They have the longest gestation period of any mammal, about twenty-two months, and are the longest living except for man. They have very thick skin (which is the meaning of "pachyderm," often used by laymen in writing about them), though this does not provide quite such protection as many believe; they suffer great discomfort from all sorts of parasites who take up residence in the deep folds and wrinkles covering much of the body, which is why elephants enjoy frequent baths and coat themselves with layers of dust or mud whenever an opportunity presents itself.

Elephants are gregarious animals, travelling in herds of up to 100, though at present these have been much reduced. Within the herds are smaller family units, each consisting of about ten who follow the leadership of an older female and show considerable affection for one another, especially new-born calves and injured or ailing members. Male Asian elephants may wander away from the herd, either alone or in groups of young "bachelors," sometimes returning to mate but at other times going to new groups for this purpose.

In the mating process, according

Opposite: Lithograph by Brodtmann, Zurich, 1827. (Courtesy of Joerg Kohler)
Above: A herd of wild elephants at Om Koi wildlife sanctuary.

to U Toke Gale, a Burmese writer, "the females, more often than not, lead the bulls up the garden path, and with a highly imaginative use of their trunks, they are capable of arousing sexual excitement

assumed the so-called "missionary position," and this added to the human qualities attributed to the animal. The explanation was anatomical rather than preference. The female's vulva is in

in the most stoical of elephants. Apart from using her trunk, the cow would occasionally rub her rump against the body of the male elephant, or playfully butt her forehead against his side, and sometimes emitting soft, seductive sounds from the throat. The male would respond to her teasing by touching the sensitive parts of her body with the tip of his trunk, but he would go about this business in silence, sedately, seriously. Sometimes, while the love-play is in full swing, high above the tree-tops would flash past a flock of screaming parakeets or parrots, and the animals would stop flapping their ears for a moment, and listen to the sound of the birds; or if in the midst of the love-play, their thoughts should suddenly turn to food, they would break off branches of fresh, green leaves and partake of these, as though the swish of birds' wings or the taste of succulent leaves was more important than all the preliminaries of love-making."

The sex life of elephants, like so much else, differs from that of other mammals and has prompted a certain amount of fantasy. Until well into the nineteenth century, for example, it was thought by many naturalists that in performing the sexual act they

the same position as the penis of the male (her two breasts are just behind the forelegs), and mating thus requires some adjustment. The male mounts from behind, but once penetration has been achieved he sinks almost to a sitting position, then gradually rises during the act with his feet resting gently on her rear; the whole process generally takes only two or three minutes and involves no other signs of movement.

The act may take place a number of times, over a period of weeks, until the female is conscious of being pregnant, after which the association gradually ends. "She will begin to cold shoulder her partner," comments Richard Carrington, "who is at first somewhat pained by her indifference, but soon accepts it with philosophical resignation. Also, it must be admitted, his eye may by then be roving toward some other seductive siren, for elephants are no more sentimental than human beings in this respect."

When a female is ready to give birth she does not seek privacy, like most other animals, but does so amidst a group of friends of her own sex, who assist her in various ways and then help care for the calf

Above: Elephants spend most their leisure time eating.

by bathing it and seeing it keeps out of danger. U Toke Gale writes, "Some people say that the expectant mother chooses an 'auntie' for her future calf; some say that the 'auntie' attaches herself to the cow who is heavy with calf. The mere existence of 'aunties' in the social system of the elephantine world has led to speculation that these self-appointed 'aunties' must either be spinsters, sterile, or too advanced in years to produce calves of their own."

The paternal instinct is less evident; indeed, in the words of one observer, "the father of an elephant calf looks upon his offspring in no other aspect than as an infernal nuisance."

They are entirely vegetarian. The Asian elephant's principal diet is grass, along with the leaves and fruit of wild bananas, bamboo shoots, and the leaves, twigs, and bark of certain trees, while by contrast the African elephant eats very little grass and prefers soft fruits and the inner bark of trees. Whatever they consume, though, they require huge quantities of it - a captive elephant can eat five hundred pounds of hay and drink sixty gallons of water in a single day, and in the wild a herd can severely damage rice fields and other human plantations that intrude on its territory. Working elephants re-

quire more food; one Burmese authority estimated that an elephant employed there in the logging industry required a daily intake of three hundred pounds for each ton that the animal weighed.

Like all animals, elephants also sleep, though precisely how much and when has given rise to considerable speculation. The truth, based on scientific studies, seems to be that they sleep lightly and only about half the time of most humans; they do it sometimes while standing and sometimes lying down, and while in the latter position they may snore. This last phenomenon apparently caused considerable excitement among researchers during a research project on the habits of circus elephants in the U.S. in the 1930s. Had the observers been familiar with ancient Thai elephant lore, especially concerning certain auspicious members of the family, they might have been surprised to learn not only that snoring was familiar in Asia but also that it could be divided into a number of categories, with the most prized, at least to properly attuned listeners, resembling the sound of musical instruments.

The elephant's most outstanding feature, both visually and in the uses to which it is put, is its long, flexible, extremely sensitive trunk, which ends in

Above: Mother elephants give close care to their calves.

one or two "fingers." With this remarkable appendage, an elephant can feed itself, suck up or expel liquids, pick up dust or sand, give a gentle caress, move extremely heavy objects, or, when so minded, kill an enemy. The tip of the trunk, the most sensitive part, is the source of the elephant's keen sense of smell, as well as the means by which it 'speaks' in a wide range of sounds to signal fear, rage, pain, pleasure, and, some think, affection. The vital role played by the trunk in almost everything the animal does perhaps explains the popular legend that elephants are mortally afraid of mice: there is no evidence for this, though quite naturally they are concerned at the prospect of these or any other small animal entering and possibly injuring the trunk, so that even in sleep they keep it carefully coiled up out of harm's way.

In some places the trunk is thought to reveal an elephant's temperament. "No superstitious Burmese," writes U Toke Gale, who worked for many years in the timber industry, "would ever think of acquiring an elephant which habitually swings his trunk from side to side like a hand rocking a cradle, or holds his trunk up in the air and then places it in the mouth as if 'he were eating clouds,' as we say in Burmese; or which constantly bobs his head up and down, as though it were pounding

paddy or glutinous rice. Purchase of such types of elephants would surely bring untold sorrow into the home of the buyer, causing unexpected loss of property, health, and even of life. It is, however, more likely that such specimens of elephants would invariably develop into dangerous man-killers."

An elephant's tail is about a foot and half long at birth and usually grows to about three and a half feet unless, as often happens, it gets bitten off in a fight. It ends in a tuft of stiff, hard bristles, which in some Asian cultures are made into rings that are believed to promote health and good fortune; they are also used as toothpicks.

Elephant toe-nails, shaped like pears, are dark-colored at birth and almost creamy-white later; nails on an African elephant are considerable larger than those of the Asian species. In ancient times, the number of nails was an important factor in evaluating an animal, and any with twenty nails, five on each foot, were said to be reserved for royal use. Such a specimen, however, was very rare; one survey of 623 Asian elephants found only three, the great majority having eighteen nails.

The life span of the elephant has been the subject of much misinformation, with various sources claiming specimens that have lived for a hundred or even more years. In fact, elephants appear to live

Above: Elephants' tails vary widely in length. *Opposite:* Elephant and mahout in Lampang province.
Following spread: Karens with elephants; most of the elephant keepers in Thailand today are Karen, the largest of the hill tribe ethnic groups.

about as long as the average man, enjoying full working strength from about twenty to forty-five and then declining. The highest verified age - that of an Asian female in the Sydney Zoo - was sixty-nine, though others are said, without proof, to have survived into their seventies and eighties. In the wild they rarely live past fifty, dying either by accident or, more prosaically, because their molar teeth have been ground down by eating tough vegetation and, being unable to find enough soft forage, they starve to death.

(According to the naturalist Richard Carrington, the age of an elephant once gave rise to an international dispute between France and Hungary. The animal in question was a bull named "Siam", on display in the Budapest Zoo. During the 1930s, the French claimed he had been given to Napoleon in Egypt by a Turkish Pasha in 1798, that he was a hundred and fifty years old, and that he rightfully belonged in Paris as a

symbol of national glory. A member of Council of the Zoological Society of London, called on for his opinion, not only denied "Siam's" supposed age but also discovered proof that the Budapest elephant had in truth come to Vienna from Siam in 1900.)

Despite its size and physical strength, the elephant is not immune from danger. Its hearing and vision are poorly developed. In the wild it may be killed by snakebite or by a variety of wild animals; according to one source, twenty-five percent of all elephant calves in Burma were killed by tigers. Even a slight injury to the trunk causes intense pain and may result in death if the animal cannot feed itself. It is subject not only to such animal ailments as anthrax (the most dreaded) and foot-and-mouth disease but also to others common to humans like diabetes, pneumonia, and mumps. Moreover, according to W.A.R. Wood, who lived for many years in northern Thailand, "their con-

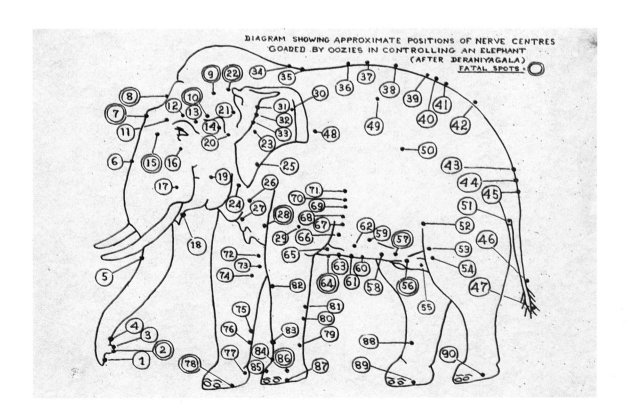

Above: Drawing from Burmese book showing elephant's control points.

dition has to be carefully watched when they are continuously employed on hard work... In their natural state they travel and feed mostly by night, and during the heat of the day they loiter about in some shady spot, smearing themselves with nice cool mud, or powdering themselves with dust. Compel them to work in hot sunshine for any long period of days, and their health is certain to suffer."

(Wood served at the British Consulate in Chiang Mai, to which a large elephant was assigned as transport. "Though a fine looking animal, he was rather liable to sunstroke and fits of giddiness, and one year I had a large straw hat made for him. He looked very raffish when wearing it, and was much jeered at by small boys in the villages through which he passed on the march; but the effect was very satisfactory.")

While certain aspects of elephant behavior remain mysterious, despite their years of association with man, others have been the subject of fairly intense study. This is especially true of domesticated Asian elephants, about which a considerable body of sometimes esoteric literature and oral traditions evolved. An ancient Indian palm-leaf manuscript, for instance, cites ninety different nerve centers scattered over the animal's body and when pressed, pulled, or struck either by a mahout's body or by a goad these produce certain reflex actions.

One center, for instance, makes the elephant twist its trunk, while another

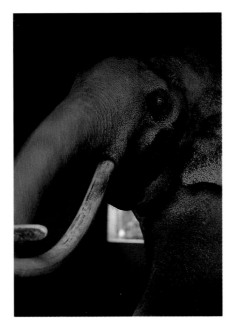

makes him straighten it. Still others cause him to kneel, move backwards or forwards, stop, bend his head to be mounted, turn around, and get up and run. Seventeen of the listed centers, according to the manuscript, can lead to the elephant's death if pressed hard enough or pierced with a spear.

Elephants can also be far more dangerous than most people who see them in zoos or demurely performing in shows might suspect. Though long trained for domestic purposes, they remain wild animals; as Richard Lair, one of the leading authorities on the Asian elephant, has noted, "In North America more zoo and circus keepers are killed annually by elephants than by all other animals combined." The chief offenders are bulls, and the cause is often a somewhat mysterious condition known as musth (a word that some think comes from Hindi and others from Singalese), when an oily, foul-smelling liquid is secreted from a gland just above the eye. This may or may not be connected with sexual functions, but it is always a signal that the animal is under severe stress and should be watched carefully. However, as Lair points out, musth is by no means the only reason for agressive behavior: "In every day management, elephants fall into three classes: some are never dangerous, some are dangerous only under very specific circumstances (in the mahout's absence, around trains, in water, etc.), and some are dangerous all of the time. The proportions

Above: A white elephant in musth at Chitralada Palace stables.

SIR JOHN BOWRING *came to Bangkok in 1855 to negotiate an historic trade treaty with King Mongkut. The following is from* The Kingdom and People of Siam, *the massive work that resulted from his trip.*

"Without the aid of the elephant, it would scarcely be possible to traverse the woods and jungles of Siam. He makes his way as he goes, crushing with his trunk all that resists his progress; over deep morasses or sloughs he drags himself on his knees and belly. When he has to cross a stream, he ascertains the depth by his proboscis, advances slowly, and when he is out of his depth he swims, breathing through his trunk, which is visible when the whole of his body is submersed. He descends into ravines impassable by man, and by the aid of his trunk ascends steep mountains. His ordinary pace is about four to five miles an hour, and he will journey day and night if properly fed. When weary, he strikes the ground with his trunk, making a sound resembling a horn, which announces to his driver that he desires repose. In Siam the howdah is a great roofed basket, in which the traveller, with the aid of his cushions, comfortably ensconces himself. The motion is disagreeable at first, but ceases to be so after a little practice."

'Caravan of Elephants Crossing Mountains of Laos', hand-colored wood-engraving, Paris, 1863. (Courtesy of Joerg Kohler)

of the classes within a group will vary somewhat according to sex-and-age structure and the quality of training, but considering every third elephant to be dangerous is a very healthy way of thinking."

W.A.R. Wood, who had frequent contact with the animals, was also quite aware of their unpredictable side. "I once saw a man killed by an elephant," he wrote in his memoirs, *Consul in Paradise*, "and once was enough. The elephant, a big tusker, was in a timber camp belonging to one of the teak firms, and was musth at the time. Its mahout went up to try to mount it, offering it a sort of cake to propitiate it. The elephant took the cake and ate it, and then suddenly seized hold of the man with its trunk, and laid him - not roughly - across its two tusks, with the trunk over him. I do not think it meant to hurt the man, and he himself kept his head and did not struggle or cry out; some of the less experienced bystanders, however, started shouting and yelling, and threw sticks, knives, and axes at the elephant, hoping to make it drop their comrade. This infuriated the elephant, which again seized the man in its trunk, and this time drew his body two or three times on to its tusks, passing them through him. It was the most fearful sight I have ever seen. The elephant finally flung away the dead and shapeless body and went quietly down to a stream nearby, where it calmly proceeded to wash its tusks."

Such hazards aside, few other animals - certainly wild ones - have been more anthropomorphized than the elephant - that is, ascribed as having distinctively human feelings and personalities. This is in spite of the fact that, in relation to its body size, its brain is comparatively small, and in the words of one authority, "There is certainly no scientific reason why the elephant should exhibit exceptional intelligence." All the same, Lair quotes a student of African elephants as commenting, "How can one do a serious study of animals that behave this way?" The literature of the Asian elephant is full of stories suggesting its sagacity and delicate sensibilities, with adjectives like 'dignified,' 'wise,' and 'affectionate' appearing regularly in descriptions; and the general public, watching them take part in circus tricks with such apparent good humor or falling in love with cartoon creations like the hapless Dumbo, almost always views them as considerably more than merely well-trained animals.

This attitude goes far back to the very beginning of man's association with elephants. Pliny, in his *Natural History*, says that "in intelligence an elephant approaches the nearest to man, and to a degree that is rare even among men, possesses notions of honesty,

AU SIAM
Capture d'un éléphant blanc

Toutes les fois que le Roi paroit, tous les Mandarins se prosterne^{nt} par respect aux piés de son Elephant. Cette planche représente ce Prince allant voir un Combat de ces animaux. On commence par sonner decertaines trompettes qui font jetter des oris horribles aux Elephans destinez pour combattre. Ils sont attachez par les piés de derriere avec de grosses cordes que plusieurs hommes tiennent afin de les retirer quand le choc est trop rude, on les laisse aprocher de telle maniere, que leurs defenses se croisent sans pouvoir se blesser. On dit qu'ils se choquent quelque fois si rudement, qu'ils se brisent les dents & en font voler les éclats de tous côtez. Le combat est plus ou moins long, selon qu'il plait au Roi, parlemoïen qu'on a d'exciter plus ou moins les Elephans. & de les retirer quand on veut.

prudence, and equity... When an elephant happens to meet a man in the desert, who is merely wandering about, the animal shows himself both merciful and kind, and even points out the way."

Simon de La Loubère, who came to the Thai capital of Ayutthaya with a French delegation toward the end of the 17th century and wrote one of the best of the early European accounts of the country, tells the story of an elephant that was punished for misbehavior by having a coconut cracked on his head. The elephant carefully collected the shell fragments and guarded them for several days between his forelegs. When an opportunity arose, he trampled on and killed the offending keeper, then deposited the fragments on the dead body. La Loubère also notes that the Siamese treated their elephants as reasonable beings, citing as evidence three of the animals that were sent as gifts by King Narai to King Louis XIV. As the animals were about to be loaded on the ship, court mandarins whispered in their ears, "Go, depart cheerfully. You will, indeed, be slaves, - but slaves to the greatest monarch in the world, whose sway is as gentle as it is glorious." (Commenting wryly on this anecdote, a later writer observed, "No doubt, this sort of invention was suited to the taste of the Grand Monarque, and the temper of the times.")

Other Europeans who were in Ayutthaya at the same time offer similar examples. Nicolas Gervais, for instance, says that when King Narai went out by land, "several of the finest elephants from His Majesty's stables are made ready at the gate of the palace to provide mounts for the greatest lords in the royal suite. The king's elephant, which is the finest and nimblest of all, bows down of its own accord as soon as it sees him approaching and it knows him so well that it will not allow anyone else, whoever he may be, to ride it." The Count Claude de Forbin writes that "these beasts are as useful to the Siamese as if they were domestic servants, especially in the care they take of their young children; for they snatch them up on their trunks when they cry, and take them to some place where they lull them asleep, and when the mother wants to have them, she demands them of the elephant, who goes and brings them to her."

Sir John Bowring, who came to Thailand in the 19th century, reports a number of colorful elephant anecdotes passed on to him. According to a Frenchman in Bangkok, he says, there was one "which was habitually sent by his keeper to collect a supply of food, which he never failed to do, and that it was divided regularly between his master and himself on his re-

Opposite: Hand-colored copper-engraving from book by Chatelain, showing King Narai's royal elephant; Paris, 1719. (Courtesy of Joerg Kohler)
Above: Drawing from manuscript book. (Private Collection)

Riding an Elephant

ISABELLA BIRD was an intrepid traveller who normally took anything difficult and unexpected in her stride. An exception was a trip she took by elephant back in 1879, recounted in her book The Golden Chersonese.

"Before I came I dreamt of howdahs and cloth of gold trappings, but my elephant had neither. In fact there was nothing grand about him but his ugliness. His back was covered with a piece of raw hide, over which were several mats, and on either side of the ridgy backbone a shallow basket, filled with fresh leaves and twigs, and held in place by ropes of rattan. I dropped into one of these baskets from the porch, a young Malay lad into the other, and my bag was tied on behind with rattan. A noose of the same with a stirrup served for the driver to mount. He was a Malay, wearing only a handkerchief and a sarong, a gossiping careless fellow, who jumped off whenever he had a chance of a talk, and left us to ourselves. He drove with a stick with a curved spike at the end of it, which, when the elephant was bad, was hooked into the membranous 'flapper,' always evoking the uprearing and brandishing of the proboscis, and a sound of urgent expostulation, which could be heard a mile off. He sat on the head of the beast, sometimes crosslegged, and sometimes with his legs behind the huge ear covers...

"This mode of riding is not comfortable. One sits facing forward with the feet dangling over the edge of the basket. This edge soon produces a sharp ache or cramp, and when one tries to get relief by leaning back on anything, the awkward rolling motion is so painful, that one reverts to the former position till it again becomes intolerable...

"Before we had travelled two hours, the great bulk of the elephant without any warning gently subsided behind, and then as gently in front, the huge, ugly legs being extended in front of him, and the man signed me to get off, which I did by getting on his head and letting myself down by a rattan rope upon the driver, who made a step of his back, for even when 'kneeling,' as this queer attitude is called, a good ladder is needed for comfortable getting off and on. While the whole arrangement of baskets was being re-rigged, I clambered into a Malay dwelling of the poorer class, and was courteously received with bananas and buffalo milk...

"When the pack was adjusted the mahout jumped on the back, and giving me his hands hauled me up over the head, after which the creature rose gently from the ground, and we went on our way.

"But the ride was 'a fearful joy,' if a joy at all! Soon the driver jumped off for a gossip and a smoke, leaving the elephant to 'gang his ain gates' for a mile or more, and he turned into the jungle, where he began to rend and tear the trees, and then going to a mud-hole he drew all the water out of it, squirted it with a loud noise over himself and his riders, soaking my clothes with it, and when he turned back to the road again, he several times stopped and seemed to stand on his head by stiffening his proboscis and leaning upon it, and when I hit him with my umbrella he uttered the loudest roar I ever heard...

"On the driver's return I had to dismount again, and this time the elephant was allowed to go and take a proper bath in a river. He threw quantities of water over himself, and took up plenty more with which to cool his sides as he went along. Thick as the wrinkled hide of an elephant looks, a very small insect can draw blood from it, and when left to himself he sagaciously plasters himself with mud to protect himself like a water buffalo. Mounting again I rode for another two hours, but he crawled about a mile an hour, and seemed to have a steady purpose to lie down. He roared whenever he was asked to go faster, sometimes with a roar of rage, sometimes in angry and sometimes in plaintive remonstrance. The driver got off and walked behind him, and then he stopped altogether. Then the man tried to pull him along by putting a hooked stick in his huge 'flapper,' but this produced no other effect than a series of howls; then he got on his head again, after which the brute made a succession of huge stumbles, each one of which threatened to be a fall, and then the driver with a look of despair got off again. Then I made signs that I would get off, but the elephant refused to lie down, and I left myself down his unshapely shoulder by a rattan rope till I could use the mahout's shoulders as steps. The baskets were taken off and left at a house, the elephant was turned loose in the jungle; I walked the remaining miles to Kwala Kangsa, and the driver carried my portmanteau! Such was the comical end of my first elephant ride."

Opposite page: Hand-colored wood-engraving; Madrid, 1883. (Courtesy of Joerg Kohler)

El autor subiendo al elefante.

turn home; and that there was another elephant, which stood at the door of the King's palace, before which a huge vessel filled with rice was placed, which he helped out with a spoon to every talapoin [Buddhist monk] who passed."

Another of the "instances of sagacity" Bowring heard was that the royal elephants were

"proud of their gorgeous trappings, and of the attentions they receive. I was assured that the removal of the gold and silver rings from their tusks was resented by the elephants as an indignity, and that they exhibited great satisfaction at their restoration. The transfer of an elephant from a better to a worse stabling is said to be accompanied with marks of displeasure."

W.A.R. Wood, not a sentimentalist on the subject, also believed that "Elephants possess some powers that seem almost uncanny. For instance, when travelling with a howdah on its back, an elephant will rarely run the howdah against an overhanging branch. Sometimes it will stop and wait if it thinks there is any danger of doing this, and if the mahout taps the branch with his goad, the elephant will pass underneath, perhaps with only half an inch to spare. Now to calculate the distance of the branch from its back merely by listening to the sound of the tap is remarkable enough, but that the elephant should allow, in addition, for an ex-

traneous object such as a howdah seems almost incredible. Yet I have seen this happen hundreds of times."

U Toke Gale recalled seeing an elderly female named Kyaungtagama ('Builder of Monasteries'), "who went around Mandalay town in the late twenties holding up all traffic - electric trams, motor cars, bicycles, pony-traps - as she shuffled across streets and from door to door to collect alms and donations for religious purposes. She would wrap her mottled trunk very carefully around a large, elaborately carved silver bowl, and would every so often shake it so that the coins inside jingled like a clash of cymbals, and at the same time, attract the pedestrians to her worthy cause. She performed all this without any word of command from her oozie [mahout] who, in fact, was seldom near his animal but away under the shade of a tama (neem) tree, chewing betel-nuts or smoking a cheroot."

A female Indian elephant acquired by the Duke of Devonshire supposedly adapted herself so well to life in England that "at a call from her keeper she would come out of her house, take up a broom, and follow his directions in sweeping the lawns or paths. She would carry pails and other objects with the pride of a dog carrying its master's gloves, and was always rewarded for her labors with a carrot."

Above: Old photograph showing howdahs on elephants (Courtesy of National Archives)
Opposite: Old photograph of carved tusks, 1890. (Courtesy of Luca Invernizzi Tettoni)

A Virtue Ascribed to an Elephant

By A. Kerr

On a recent tour in Songkla Province I had with me two elephants, one of which was a fine tusker. One morning, in the sub-district of Natawi, we were in a small village, just preparing to start on our day march, when a woman of the village came up with a water bottle, a brass bowl and a taper. She spoke a few words to the head elephant-man, and then gave him these articles. The head-man lighted the taper and stuck it on the edge of the brass bowl; he then passed up the water-bottle to the mahout sitting on the tusker's neck. The mahout poured the water out of the bottle on to the top of the elephant's head in such a way that it ran down the left side of the face on to the left tusk. The head-man held the brass bowl under the tip of the left tusk to receive the water. When the water had finished running the head-man handed back the water bottle and the bowl, with the water it contained, to the woman. On making inquiries, I was informed that the woman had a child who was ill with fever, and that she proposed to bathe the child in the water that had run down the elephant's head and along its left tusk. Further, I was told that such water was often efficacious in curing fever; but it was only certain elephants that could endow the water with this power. The elephant in question was a great grandfather, and on that account possessed this virtue.

Reprinted with permission from Journal of the Siam Society, *1928.*

And D.H. Lawrence, after seeing elephants perform in a circus in Sri Lanka, was moved to write this poem:

The huge old female on the drum
shuffles gingerly round
and smiles; the vastness of her
elephant antiquity
is amused.

"For describing true domestic animals," Richard Lair writes, "the word 'temperament' is allowable when speaking either of behavioral traits presumed common to a breed or the typical behavior of a specific dog or horse, etc. When used with people, 'temperament' clearly implies the nature of an individual personality. Perhaps the word is inappropriate for domesticated elephants, which are true wild animals, but somehow 'temperament' remains the most fitting word to describe what makes the behavior of one domesticated elephant different from any another."

There are a number of specific differences between the Asian and the African elephant. The Asian species is somewhat smaller in overall size, with a less domed forehead, and more complex teeth; its smooth trunk has a single fingerlike process at the tip rather than two; the ears are conspicuously different, being much larger on the African elephant. Only the males in Asia develop tusks, which are on average about five feet long, a pair weighing about seventy pounds; both male and female African elephants have tusks, which are generally longer and thicker. (Not all Asian males have tusks; some, known as Sidaw in Thailand, are born without them. However, notes W.A.R. Wood, "Sidaw elephants are in no way lacking in virility; on the contrary, some experts say that they are particularly fond of the other sex. A Sidaw elephant belonging to the British Consulate in Chiang Mai became in a few years the father of five calves, two of which were tuskers.") Four geographical types of Asian elephant have been recognized - the Indian, Sri Lankan, Malayan, and the Sumatran - and within these there are also slight physical differences; Sumatran elephants, for example, are of slighter build, and tusks are rarer on Sri Lankan males.

Opposite: Illustration from old manuscript book featuring yantras (magic formulas) for taming elephants.
Above: Old illustration showing elephant gear for fighting a tiger. (Both courtesy of National Library)

There is a common belief that the African elephant is untameable, but this is not supported by history or experience. In fact, mainly because of geographical proximity, it was the African elephant that first made an impact on western Europe, figuring in such famous incidents as Hannibal's epic crossing of the Alps with thirty-seven of the animals in 218 BC; most of the elephants used by Caesar and other Roman leaders were probably also African. King Leopold II of Belgium put local elephants to work in the Congo in the late 19th century, after an earlier experience of importing some Asian ones from Sri Lanka failed. Finally, the famous Jumbo, whose purchase from the London Zoo by the showman P.T. Barnum caused a storm of protest by animal lovers in England, was of African origin.

On the other hand, there is no doubt that the elephant has played a much more varied role in Asian life. To tribes scattered throughout the jungles of Africa the animal was only occasionally a useful beast of burden (most domestication was confined to the northwestern part of the continent), more often a convenient source of meat and lucrative ivory. Due to the relatively small population, elephants and men kept their distance from one another and there was less opportunity for frequent interaction or for a deep spiritual bond to be forged between them.

It was very different in Asia. The last wild elephants disappeared from Southern China around the tenth century, mainly due to the growth of population, but large numbers continued to be found in India, Sri Lanka, Sumatra, Malaysia, Thailand, and Indo-China. In nearly all these countries, a complex relationship between man and elephant was established very early, based partly on the practical role played by the animal and partly on its symbolic significance. Over the centuries, this came to exert a powerful influence over a vast cultural range extending from art to religion, from the conduct of war to countless aspects of daily life.

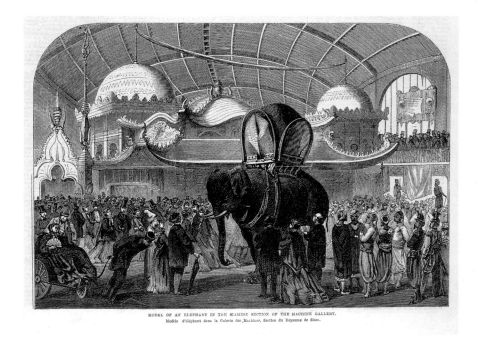

MODEL OF AN ELEPHANT IN THE SIAMESE SECTION OF THE MACHINE GALLERY.
Modèle d'éléphant dans la Galerie des Machines, section du Royaume de Siam.

Above: Model of an elephant in the Siamese section of an exhibition; hand-colored wood-engraving from *The Illustrated London News*, 1867. (Courtesy of Joerg Kohler)
Opposite: Karen hilltribe with elephants in Um Phang, Tak province.

Elephant Lore

A Miscellany of Odd Facts, Beliefs, and Customs Concerning the Asian Elephant

A medieval Indian manuscript includes the following elephant superstitions:
A dumb elephant will cause a shortage of rain.
A deaf elephant will cause loss of wealth.
An elephant with constantly watering eyes will bring sorrow and misfortune to the owner and his family.
An elephant with conspicuous testicles is mean.
Possession of an elephant with a spotted trunk will bring death to a king.
An elephant which has any limb or organ that is out of proportion is unlucky.

■

The Kui people, who have long captured and owned elephants, traditionally use certain of their products as medicine. The hair is used as a toothpick and believed to counter poisonous food. Elephant excrement, wrapped in cloth and pressed against the forehead, lowers fever, while mixed with water and drunk it relieves malaria. The oily substance secreted when an elephant is in musth can be used as a love potion.

■

From an article on elephants by F.H. Giles in the Journal of the Siam Society *in 1930:*
"So deeply has the elephant entered into the life of Asia that it has been called on to take part in the ceremony of praying for rain, which is performed in the seventh month of the year (June-July)... Two 'musth' elephants would be tied to posts with strong ropes of sufficient length to allow their tusks to meet, but not long enough to allow them to inflict wound. These animals, being much excited by their 'musth' condition, would rush at each other in an attempt to fight, their tusks would clash, giving forth a loud sound. The animal which succeeded in forcing its tusks between those of its opponent and with this leverage, in raising the other's head, was deemed victor. The animals would then be separated and the mahouts indulge in a competitive dance and exchange of views regarding the other's skill and courage. This false combat, known as *bamru-gna* (clashing of tusks), would be fought three times, followed by the drama and word war on the part of the mahouts. The movements, rhythm, and postures of the dance followed a set form."

■

An old Malay belief holds that "a stirring rod of ivory will become dusky if poison should have been put in the food."

■

In selecting elephants that would become the personal property of the King of Burma, 315 points were considered by a high official called the Sin-wun. Most of these concerned the shape and growth of the tusks, the formation of the spinal ridge, movements of the ears and tail, sleeping and eating habits, and skin texture. There were 42 points that revealed physical abnormality, any of which rendered an animal unsuited to royal service.

Opposite: 19th century illustrated horoscope book.

Above: An annual ordination ceremony at Ta Klang village in Surin involves a procession with as many as 100 elephants.
Following spread: Painted wooden panels originally from a temple in Phrae now installed at Mae Fah Luang Foundation in Chiang Rai.

The Thai Elephant in History

The first recorded elephant in Thai history occurs in a stone inscription traditionally thought to have been composed in 1292 by order of King Ramkamhaeng the Great of Sukhothai. Indeed, elephants of various kinds - tame and wild, sacred and mundane - figure all through this famous evocation of life in an idyllic kingdom.

"When I was nineteen years old," states the King in the official translation of the inscription, prepared to celebrate the 700th anniversary of the Thai alphabet, "Khun Sam Chon, the ruler of Muang Chot, came to raid Muang Tak. My father went to fight Khun Sam Chon on the left; Khun Sam Chon drove forward on the right. Khun Sam Chon charged in; my father's men fled in confusion. I did not flee. I mounted my elephant, named Bekhpon, and pushed him ahead in front of my father. I fought an elephant duel with Khun Sam Chon. I fought Khun Sam Chon's elephant, Mas Muang by name, and beat him. Khun Sam Chon fled. Then my father named me Phra Ramkamhaeng because I fought Khun Sam Chon's elephant."

Later he informs the reader that "when I went hunting elephants and

caught some, either by lasso or by driving them into a corral, I brought them to my father." Moving further in time, he extols the virtues of the kingdom he has inherited and now rules, in a passage that forms part of the education of every Thai schoolchild:

"In the time of King Ramkamhaeng, this land of Sukhothai is thriving. There are fish in the water and rice in the fields. The lord of the realm does not levy toll on his subjects. They are free to lead their cattle and ride their horses or engage in trade; whoever wants to trade in elephants, does so; whoever wants to trade in horses, does so; whoever wants to trade in silver or gold, does so. When any commoner or man of rank dies, his estate - his elephants, wives, children, relatives, rice granaries, retainers, and groves of areca and betel - is left entirely to his son."

And still later, describing the festivals and rituals of Sukhothai, he writes, "On the day of the new moon and the day of the full moon, when the white elephant named Rucagri has been decked out with howdah and tasseled head cloth, and always with gold on both tusks, King Ramkamhaeng mounts him, rides away to the Arannika [sanctuary near the city] to pay homage to the Buddha, and then returns."

Preceding spread: The stupa of Wat Chedi Si Hong in Sukhothai is butressed by *garudas* (mythical birds) mounted on elephants.
Opposite: Wat Chang Lom ('the temple circled with elephants') at Si Satchanalai,
built towards the end of the 13th century. *Above:* Early 19th century wood panels painted in folk style at
Wat Phra That Lampang Luang in northern Thailand.

It is clear from this that long before the inscription was composed, the elephant was already firmly established as a vital part of Thai life. The main elements are there, obviously so familiar to any reader they needed no further explanation - the use of elephants in war, the specific names of those ridden by famous leaders, the capture of wild elephants and trade in the animals, the role of the sacred white elephant in ritual, even the suggestion that, in terms of importance, elephants rank ahead of wives and children when it comes to the distribution of a man's estate. Only the claim that King Ramkamhaeng rode a white elephant might seem unusual to later rulers of Ayutthaya and Bangkok, for according to most accounts such specimens were regarded as far too lofty to bear even the greatest of human beings.

Precisely when the Asian elephant was first tamed and put to use at the service of man is debatable, but it was certainly before the earliest documented Indian civilizations, about 4,000 years ago. Some scholars believe the process could have developed elsewhere as well, perhaps simultaneously, perhaps even earlier, in other areas where wild elephants were abundant, such as Sri Lanka, Burma, Thailand, Cambodia, Laos, and Vietnam. In any event it is from the Indus Valley, in an area now part of Pa-

kistan, that clear evidence of domestication first appears in the form of seals and various other objects. Later there were texts, obviously derived from oral tradition, on methods of capturing and taming wild elephants, on the relationship between the animals and their mahouts, or trainers, on their symbolic association with royalty and religion, and on their use for a wide variety of practical purposes.

The use that has probably most captured popular imagination was in war, though this actually accounted for a relatively small part of the total number of domesticated elephants at any moment in history. Alexander the Great encountered the phenomenon in 326 BC when his opponent, the Indian King Porus, massed 200 elephants, 50,000 infantrymen, 4,000 cavalrymen, and 300 war chariots on the banks of the Hydaspes River. The infantry and cavalry posed no serious problem; the elephants, though, terrified the Macedonian troops with their size and ferocity. According to one account, "The most dismal thing of all was when these animals took up the armed soldiers with their trunks and delivered them up to their governors on their backs." Victory was finally achieved, and eighty of the elephants were captured, but only at the cost of heavy losses that may, in the opinion of some, have prompted the Macedonians to refuse to follow Alexander into the

Opposite top: Prehistoric earthenware vessel excavated in northeast Thailand; height 10.5 cm.
Opposite bottom: Unglazed earthenware about 3,000 years old from Lopburi; height 14 cm. (Both Collection of Prof. Arun Chaiseri)
Above: Water well with elephant figures in Sipscng Panna district in southern China where the domestication of elephants was once a common practice. *Following spread:* Prehistoric rock paintings at Pha Taem in Ubon province feature elephants and other anima s.

heart of India. (Alexander, it might be noted, was so impressed by the bravery of his opponent that he allowed him to retain his kingdom. A medal showing Alexander wearing an elephant headdress is believed by some to have been made to commemorate the battle.)

Rulers in many parts of Asia, including Thailand, measured their power by the number of elephants they could muster on a battlefield. In the words of Maurice Collis, these superbly trained animals, sometimes clad in leather or metal armor, bristling with weapons, were very different from "the poor clownish creatures of the circus, or the brokenhearted beasts at the zoo to whom an infant may safely offer a bun." Instead, this was "an animal trained to be obediently ferocious, in battle to wield a mighty sword, and, as an executioner, to kill men by tossing, trampling, and rending them. Such monsters relished a bran mash flavored with babies."

Another writer notes that the elephant was "the forerunner of the modern armored tank, and like the tank, it had a psychological as well as a physical effect on the enemy. It did not become obsolete until the introduction of firearms gradually made it more of a liability than an asset. This was not because the elephant was especially vulnerable to firearms, but because it was reduced to a panic by the noise of their explosion; it would then be as likely to stampede through its own lines as to charge the opposing army." Even in the mid-eighteenth century, however, by which time guns were common in the region, elephants still appeared in battle. Attacking Ayutthaya in 1764, a Burmese King reportedly used 5,000 with wooden castles on their backs, from which long guns were fired; the effort failed, however, and it was to be three years before the capital finally fell and was reduced to ruins.

Elephants were the first to charge in a battle, often led by the king on his own special mount, carrying a saber and directing the army's movements by means of a signaller higher up on the animal, while another man steered with the aid of a hooked instrument. More than two centuries before King Ramkamhaeng's inscription, Thais (identifed as "Sayam") appeared as foot-soldiers on a bas relief at Angkor Wat, walking in a procession that includes a war elephant.

Some of the most noted figures in Thai history achieved their reknown in epic battles. Six months after King Mahachakrapat came to the throne in 1549, a Burmese army advanced over the Three Pagoda Pass and laid seige to Ayutthaya. The king rode out on a sortie, accompanied by two sons as well as Queen Suriyothai and Princess Tepsatri, all in warrior's dress and on their elephants. When the king found himself in difficulties, Queen Suriyothai drove her elephant between him and his pursuers and saved him, though at the cost

Preceding spread: Stone lintel at Prasat Hin Phanom Rung portraying a battle scene between two clans. *Above:* Bas relief at Angkor Wat depicting Siamese soldiers. *Opposite:* Detail of mural at Wat Phra Kaew Wang Na, Bangkok.

of her life. It was the first time a Thai queen had appeared on a battlefield, and it earned Queen Suriyothai a monument and a lasting reputation as one of the country's great heroines.

During King Mahachakrapat's reign, more than 300 elephants were captured and trained for warfare; seven proved to be white elephants, leading people to call him "Lord of the White Elephant" and also inspiring the envy of neighboring Burma, a story told in the next chapter.

Another historic encounter on elephant back took place in 1593, when King Naresuan killed the Burmese Crown Prince in a duel near the present-day city of Suphanburi, thus insuring Thai independence for the following generation. A leather cap that he was wearing at the time, a crescent cut out of it during the fight, as well as his sword, became part of the royal regalia and remained so until the de-

struction of Ayutthaya in 1767; the battle itself is commemorated by a modern monument at Don Chedi in Suphanburi.

Richard Lair notes that the term "war elephant" is somewhat misleading. Only a few of the thousands mentioned in chronicles actually took part in battle, the great majority serving as transport for men and equipment. Indeed, transportation and heavy physical labor were the principal uses of elephants. African elephants were commonly killed for their meat or ivory, or simply for sport - big-game hunters of less than a century ago prided themselves on their skill at bringing down a big bull with a single shot - but this was rare in Asia. Ivory was obtained either from living animals, by cropping the tusks, or from those who had died naturally. Instead, elaborate methods evolved to capture live wild elephants and then to train them for service to man.

Above: Painted wooden panels at Wat Phra That Lampang Luang depicting a battle scene.
Opposite: Detail of colored-lacquer cabinet showing elephants in warfare. (Wang Chankasem Museum, Ayutthaya)

The Elephant in War

THE following is from Hindu Manners, Customs, and Ceremonies, *written at the beginning of the nineteenth century by the Abbe J.A. Dubois. Though it is about war elephants in ancient India, most of it would apply to Thailand as well.*

"In the first line [of attack] came the elephants. It is certain that these animals carried castles or howdahs on their backs, containing several men armed with javelins. But I think it would be wrong to suppose that these castles or howdahs were of any great size, as might be imagined from certain illustrations. Like those which may still be found in the present day amongst the armies of some Eastern princes, these towers or howdahs resembled large boxes without lids, as long and as broad as a large bed, placed crosswise on the back of the elephant, and capable of holding six or seven archers when sitting in Oriental fashion. Though an elephant is very strong, so as to be able to carry two small cannons and their carriages, there is nevertheless a limit to its powers; and naturally a much larger erection, with a still larger number of men in it, would be a burden, under which even an elephant would succumb. And there is another point, namely, the difficulty of fixing a lofty structure with any degree of security on an elephant's back, a difficulty which would be rendered practically insurmountable by the brusque movements and rolling gait of the animal. Be this as it may, elephants in days gone by were formidable adversaries amongst these half-disciplined nations. They broke the ranks, frightened the horses, trampled the soldiers underfoot; and at the same time it was very difficult to wound them, on account of their hard and horny epidermis."

LES ÉVÉNEMENTS DE SIAM
(L'armée siamoise en marche)

Opposite: 'War Elephant', hand-colored wood-engraving; Paris, 1875.
Above: 'Siamese Army on the March', colored zinc etching from *Le Petit Journal*; Paris 1893. (Both courtesy of Joerg Kohler)

ELEPHANT AVEC SA CHAISE POUR LA PRINCESSE REYNE. | ELEPHANT AVEC SA CHAISE POUR LES ETRANGERS.

Chasse des Elephans.

Pour prendre ces animaux, on fait durant la nuit une grande enceinte d'un quarré long, qui est quelquefois de vingt lieües. On la borde de deux rangs de feux, qui regnen tout autour sur deux lignes à quatre ou cinq pas de distance les uns des autres. De grandes lanternes disposées d'espace en espace, font la distinction des quartiers que commandent differens chefs avec certain nombre d'Elephans de guerre & de chasse armez comme les Soldats. On tire ensuite de tems en tems quelques pieces de campagne pour etonner les Elefans Jauvages parce bruit & par ces feux. A mesure qu'on en aproche, on leur jette des coulans & des filets, & quand ils sont bien attachez, on les met chacun entre deux Elephàns de guerre qui les domptent à grands coups de trompe, & qui les font obeir jusqu'à ce qu'ils Joient entierement aprivoisez.

In the autumn of 1685, a splendid French embassy arrived in Ayutthaya, bringing a personal letter from Louis XIV to King Narai. It was a significant step in a process that was intended to bring about a grand alliance and, not coincidentally, offset pressures from other European powers like England and Holland; instead, it exacerbated long-simmering tensions that just over two years later would explode in violence and see the expulsion of the French and most other foreigners. For the moment, though, all seemed to be going well. "They were the first European gentlemen of quality the Siamese had ever seen," Maurice Collis has written. They looked at the extraordinary scenes around them not merely with curiosity, like the traders and missionaries who had preceded them, but also with a high degree of sophistication and considerable perception, all of which they put into the books that many of them later wrote about their experiences.

Elephants, inevitably, figured largely in these impressions - not because they were strange, for by that time both Asian and African elephants were well known in Europe, but because of the extraordinary settings in which they appeared. "At four in the afternoon," wrote the Abbé de Choisy in a letter, "the King left the palace on his elephant. All the streets were flanked by guards on foot and horseback. Each infantryman had a helmet, a breastplate, and a gilded shield. The Moors were on well-appointed horses and looked good. The mandarins went before and after the King, with their ceremonial bonnets shaped like pyramids surrounded by several rings of gold,

each according to his rank. After the King walked the parade elephant, carrying a solid gold chain. Then came the young mandarin whom the King treats like his son; he alone raised his head; all the rest had their heads lowered over the neck of their elephants. I assure you this procession was most noble and most singular, and I think the Pharaoh on the banks of the Nile must have paraded in similar pomp."

Godlike in his Ayutthaya palace, where every move was surrounded by ritual and intrigue, King Narai was fond of escaping for long periods to a more comfortable retreat at Lopburi (called Louvo by Europeans), a day's journey to the north. Here he had a semi-European palace with a pretty garden; even more to his liking, the surrounding area was full of wild animals available for hunting.

"His favorite pastime is hunting tigers and elephants," wrote a Jesuit priest named Nicolas Gervaise, who lived in Siam for about five years, "and this he does all the time that he is at Louvo, that is to say from November to the end of July or the beginning of August. Never has there been a prince more skilful or fortunate than he. Never a year passes during which he fails to take more than three hundred elephants. He reserves the most beautiful for his own use and presents those who are less so to the mandarins who are in favor or who have rendered him the greatest services. The rest he sells to foreigners, who send them to the Mogul and to neighboring kingdoms."

Wild elephants were plentiful in the central plains at that time - indeed, even in the late nineteenth century herds could be

Preceding spread: Remains of the elephant stables at King Narai's summer palace in Lopburi built in 1666.
Opposite: Hand-colored copper-engraving showing royal elephants of King Narai, from a book by Chatelain; Paris, 1719. (Courtesy of Joerg Kohler)

The Kui

A large number - perhaps the majority - of the elephant owners and mahouts in Thailand today belong to one of several minority groups. The best known of these, living largely in northeastern provinces near the Cambodian border, are known in Thai as Suay but to themselves as Kui (which simply means "the people").

Most authorities believe the Kui came to the region long before either the Khmer or the Thai, possibly, in the opinion of one, "the descendants of an ancient Veddoid migration eastward from the Indian subcontinent." They became noted for their expertise at capturing wild elephants, hunting in open areas and snaring their prey by slipping a noose on one of the hind feet, and developed a special language - called *phasaa phii paa*, or "forest spirit language" in Thai - that was used only when engaged in this dangerous work. Teams riding tame elephants would follow the wild herds and noose selected animals, usually young ones, which were then secured by other men who followed on foot. By this means they captured twenty to thirty elephants a year, selling most of them to Burmese, Shan, and northern Thais for work in the timber concessions of the north.

By the early 1950s, however, the Kui elephant-catching days were drawing to a close, if they were not already over. The forests and grasslands of the two main provinces where they lived were declining rapidly and, with them, the herds of wild animals, which had once included not only elephants but also two species of rhinoceros, water buffalo, gaur, and kouprey. In 1957, the Thai government forbid hunters to cross the border into Cambodia in pursuit of any that remained in that country. Increasingly, too, the Kui became more assimilated, forgetting many of their tribal traditions in the process. A number, however, have retained their fabled elephant-keeping skills, taking part in the popular Surin Elephant Roundup and, despite a ban by municipal authorities, seasonally bringing their charges down to Bangkok to earn desperately-needed money by selling food to be given to the elephants or allowing people to acquire luck by walking under the animal's belly three times.

Richard Lair has written, "The supreme irony of these men and elephants coming to Bangkok between rice harvests is that as recently as thirty years ago they would have trekked into the forests of Cambodia to capture wild elephants to rough-break and sell."

Below: Manuscript painting depicting an elephant hunt.
Opposite: Mud-mee silk with an elephant and rider motif, woven by Kui women in Surin. (Private Collection)

found only twenty or thirty miles away from Bangkok - and elephant hunting was a hereditary profession, its methods passed down from father to son, with young would-be hunters starting out on mundane camp chores and familiarizing themselves with the ways of tame elephants. It was also dangerous; an enraged wild bull could be a fearful adversary, and many hunters failed to return alive. For this reason, solemn ceremonies were performed to invoke spiritual assistance before each hunt, protective amulets were carried, and the men involved assumed an almost monklike virtue. Even their wives had to observe certain proprieties while they were away - remaining chaste, for example, sleeping on a bare floor, wearing no jewelry, and showing no overt sign of happiness - to prove their sincerity.

The rewards, though, could be considerable. A master hunter, that is one who captured at least fifteen elephants, was a figure of high status, likely to receive valuable marks of esteem from the king and perhaps even rise into the warrior ranks; Phra Petracha, who seized the throne when King Narai fell mortally ill, had been head of the Krom Chang, or Elephant Department, earlier in his career.

Hunting methods varied in different parts of the country, sometimes involving the capture of individual animals, sometimes using the natural

instinct of herds to drive large numbers of them into a kraal, or stockade, especially built for the purpose. Guy Tachard, another Jesuit who came with the French delegation and witnessed a hunt near Lopburi, wrote of the latter method:

"Huntsmen go into the woods, mounted on she-elephants which are trained to the game, and cover themselves with leaves of trees that they may not be seen by wild elephants. When they have got pretty far in the forest, where they think some elephants may be, they make the females give some noises that are proper to attract the males, who presently answer by dreadful roarings. Then the huntsmen, perceiving them at a vast distance, return back again, and gently lead the females toward [the stockade]. The wild elephants never fail to follow them."

Tachard watched the training of one particular male who was lured into captivity by this means:

"So soon as he was there the bar was shut; the females kept on their way across the amphitheater and at one another's tails passed along the little alley that was at the other end... Some Siamese provoked the wild elephant by clapping their hands and crying *pat*, *pat*, others pricked him with sharp, pointed poles, and when they were pursued by him, slipped between the pillars and hid themselves behind the palisades bank

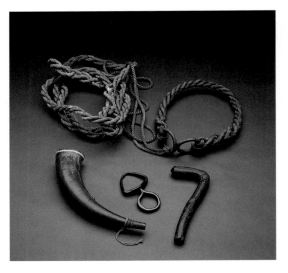

Above: Ropes, nooses, and other items used by the Kui people on expeditions to capture elephants in the forests of Cambodia. (Royal Elephant National Museum)
Opposite: Re-enactment of an elephant roundup in Ayutthaya. *Following spread:* Old photograph showing elephant roundup at the kraal in Ayutthaya, 1900. (Courtesy of Luca Invernizzi Tettoni)

Chasse Pour Prendre les Elephans

On fait Une estacade ou Palissade degros pieux ou arbres entiers dont l'enceinte est triangulaire et a quelque fois deux Lieües de tour ou de Circuit on laisse la baze de ce triangle ouvert pour la fermer quand on veut, on a des pieux tous prest a terre, Vis avis de cette enceinte on fait dans la forest Une battüe deplusieures milliers d'hommes a quelques lieües de Cette palissade, ils font Un grand Cercle et avec des tambours des trompetes et des mousquets ils epouvantent et font fuir les Elephans Sauvages, les Conduisants vers l'estacade ou les ayant reduits ils les renferment avec les pieux preparez et pour les prendre et les apriuoiser on a Une porte a l'endroit le plus estroit et l'on y fait entrer Un Elephant docile qui va badiner avec le premier elephant sauvage auquel on jete Une Corde au Col et l'on le joint a l'elephant domestique on les fait sortir de cette enceinte et l'on les liy ainsy jusqu'a ce qu'ils Soient aprivoisez

Elephants in the Time of King Narai

In the early 18th century, a number of watercolors showing Thai elephants were produced in France. Now at the Bibliothèque Nationale in Paris, these were obviously inspired by accounts brought back by the various Frenchmen who came during the reign of King Narai. One, reproduced on pages 8-9, shows the royal enclosure, where "every elephant has its own stable of brick or bamboo and several attendants." Another, shown on the following pages is entitled "A Hunt to Capture Elephants" and depicts one of the huge stockades built during the roundups described by several of the visitors; the caption says in part, "A corral or stockade is fashioned from large stakes or entire trees, forming a triangular enclosure....A shelter for several thousand men is built in the forest a few leagues from this stockade. They fan out into a huge circle and with drums, trumpets and muskets they terrify the wild elephants and put them to flight, all the while driving them towards the stockade, where....they confine them with stakes specially designed for capturing and taming them. There is a gate at the narrowest point and a docile elephant is led in to distract the first wild elephant so that it may be roped and tied to it....". A third drawing, below, shows a group of spectators watching a fight between three elephants and a tiger. "The elephant sometimes wraps its trunk around the middle of the tiger's body and flings it into the air when its handler or rider orders it to do so."

combat.

D'un tigre auec des eléphants quelque fois l'on voit. L'éléphant prendre auec sa trompe —
Le tigre par le milieu du corps et le jetter en l'air; quand son cornac ou l'homme
qui est dessus lui ordonne il le foule auec les pieds ou le reçoit sur ses dents. Le —
tigre tâche principalement de prendre la trompe auec ses griffes et l'éléphant

which the elephant could not break through. At length, after having pursued several of the huntsmen, he made at one single man with a great deal of fury. The man ran into the alley and the elephant after him; but as soon as he was within he was taken, for the man having made his escape, they let fall two [barriers], one before and the other behind the elephant, so that being powerless to go forward or backwards he struggled prodigiously and made terrible cries. They endeavored to pacify him by throwing buckets of water over his body, rubbing him with leaves, pouring oil upon his ears, and they brought tame elephants both males and females to him who caressed him with their trunks. In the meantime, they fastened ropes under his belly and to his hind feet, so that they might pull him out from there, and they persisted in throwing water upon his trunk and body to cool him....

"They left him there until the next day that he might spend his anger; but while he tormented himself around that pillar, a Brahmin (that is to say one of the Indian priests who are numerous in Siam), clothed in white and mounted on another elephant, drew nigh and... sprinkled him with a certain water consecrated after their manner, which he carried in a vessel of gold. They believe that ceremony makes the elephant lose his natural fierceness, and fits him to serve the King. The following day he began to go with the rest and in a fortnight's time is fully tamed."

At least one writer, Richard Carrington, finds this method of using tame females "somewhat reprehensible." After describing its operation, he concludes, "One would think that such an experience of this kind would be sufficient to put an elephant off female society for life, but such is the forgiving nature of the animals that the bull is soon working alongside the very cows who have brought about his downfall, and even perhaps showing his forgiveness by bringing one of them to bed of a fine calf."

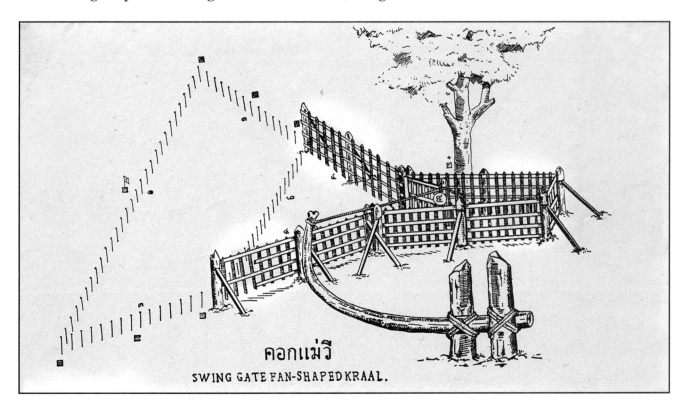

คอกแม่วี
SWING GATE FAN-SHAPED KRAAL.

Above: Drawing of a kraal. (Reprinted with permission from the *Journal of The Siam Society,* vol. XXV, 1932)

Another kraal, near the ruins of Ayutthaya, still stands in the same site where a similar structure was built at the time of the city's establishment in the mid-14th century. It is a square enclosure of stout teak pillars,

then strongly bound and conducted to the stables."

This kraal was still in use in the early years of the present century, when King Chulalongkorn occasionally staged elephant roundups for the amusement of

sunk in the ground about two feet apart, and surrounded in turn by a thick wall; entry is by means of a bottleneck just large enough for the captive elephants to enter one by one. On the opposite side is a pavilion where the King sat to watch the proceedings, and on one side a small pavilion where the hunters asked for spiritual protection.

Sir John Bowring cites an account from a man who visited the remains of Ayutthaya in 1855 and who reported that despite the old capital's destruction a century before the custom continued. Elephants, he said, "abound in the neighborhood of the city," and once a year captured specimens were gathered in the stockade. "On this occasion the kings, and a large concourse of nobles, assemble together to witness the proceedings... The wild elephants are then driven in by the aid of tame males of a very large size and great strength, and the selection takes place. If an animal which is wanted escapes from the kraal, chase is immediately made after it by a tame elephant, the driver of which throws a lasso to catch the feet of the fugitive. Having effected this, the animal on which he rides leans itself with all its power the opposite way, and thus brings the other violently to the ground. It is

distinguished visitors. One, for example, was held in 1891 in honor of the future Tsar Nicholas II of Russia, then Crown Prince; a particularly fierce bull, which put up such a fight it took all day to lasso him, was given the name of "Tsarvitch", while the mother of a baby presented to the prince protested so pathetically that the gift was graciously refused, winning cheers from the spectators.

Though by that time most of the elephants used were at least partially tamed, it was still a thrilling spectacle for both Thais and foreigners. "In Bangkok all the Government offices are closed, and everyone goes up to Ayutthaya," wrote P.A. Thompson, an Englishman who went to one of the roundups in 1905. "The trains are packed to overflowing, and the houseboats along the river recall, in a small way, the scene at Henley Regatta."

Thompson saw the final drive toward the kraal, when the elephants "were already half-way across the plain, moving forward in a compact black mass guarded by the tame tuskers on every side. Each of the tuskers was ridden by a mahout and an elephant catcher, wearing blue uniforms and broad-brimmed sun helmets. As the herd approached the river

Above: Colored zinc-etching depicting the elephant kraal at Ayutthaya. (Courtesy of Joerg Kohler)

the crowd scattered from before them, taking refuge behind the flanking lines of tame elephants. Straight on the leader went, down the bank, and waded out into the river. Then followed a fine sight as the great herd hesitated for an instant on the brink, and poured over the edge in a black wave, two hundred and fifty of them, slipping and sliding down the steep bank in a cloud of dust, with trumpetings and squeals. Soon they were all swimming, keeping so closely together that they formed one black patch upon the water, while the tuskers preserved their positions on every side. As they swam they held the tips of their trunks above the surface, while the mahouts, upon the backs of the tame elephants, knelt or stood upright. After gaining the other side the herd was allowed to rest for a while, and the hot, thirsty animals revelled in the shallow water, taking deep draughts and squirting streams over each other in excess of joy."

The last official round-up in the Ayutthaya kraal took place a year after the one Thompson saw; another, largely staged and ceremonial, was held in 1938. The last legal capture of wild Thai elephants was in the early 1970s, though there have been scattered examples in later years.

The captured elephants of the past were subjected to further training, essentially aimed at breaking their wild spirit and teaching them to respond to various words of command, most of them monosyllabic. Both tough and gentle techniques were employed in the process, though experience showed that the latter produced a better-tempered, more tractable elephant. In the mid-nineteenth century, drawing on much older sources, Sir John Bowring wrote, "The process of taming commences by keeping them for several days without food; then a cord is passed around their feet, and they are attached to a strong column. The delicacies of which they are most fond are then supplied them, such as sugar canes, plantains, and fresh herbs; and at the end of a few days the animal is domesticated and resigned to his fate." Then, and still today, a single mahout was usually assigned to each animal, forging

Above: 'Wild elephants escape from kraal of Ayutthaya during flood', hand-colored wood engraving
from *Le Tour de Monde*; Paris, 1863. (Courtesy of Joerg Kohler)
Opposite top: Interior of the Royal Elephant National Museum dominated by a model of a white elephant.
Opposite bottom: Platform for mounting elephants in the Grand Palace compound.

a close bond that often lasted for the lifetime of either man or animal, with the mahout going wherever his elephant went. Training, like hunting, was an hereditary profession, often extending over several generations and bringing a certain social status with it.

The strongest and most adept elephants were usually placed in royal service for transport or use in war. The very best - which had to possess certain characteristics ranging from physical appearance to temperament - became the King's personal property and when not required for combat or some ceremonial procession lived in a great deal of style. Jacques de Coutre, a merchant from Bruges, visited Ayutthaya in 1596, during the reign of King Naresuan, and was much impressed by these arrangements:

"The palace is surrounded by stables where live the favorite elephants ridden by the king when he goes out. I went to see them out of curiosity. They were in great number, and two among them were particularly valued and pampered... Each one had its silk cushion, and they slept on it as if they were small dogs. It is easy to imagine the size of cushions made for elephants of six yards or more. They were fastened with chains as heavy as door-chains,

plated with gold... Even the tassels were of silk, and each one of them had six very large bowls of gold. It is obvious that they had to be huge; their thickness was that of a four real piece. Some contained oil to grease their skins; others were filled with water for sprinkling; others served for eating, others for drinking, others for urinating and defecating. The elephants were indeed so well trained that they got up from their beds when they felt the urge to urinate or defecate. Their attendants understood at once and handed them the bowls. And they kept their lodgings always very sweet-smelling and fumigated with benzoin and other fragrant substances."

The writer and translator Michael Smithies warns that de Coutre's account must be treated with some caution, as its veracity cannot be checked. It does seem possible that the elephants he saw were special ones, perhaps belonging to some auspicious category below that of the rare albino regarded as sacred. Other accounts, however, among them the caption for the French watercolor of the royal stables mentioned above, agree that the royal elephants enjoyed a status far above that of others.

Above: Mural at Phra Thinang Phutthaisawan at the National Museum depicting a royal stable.
Opposite: Phra Thinang Aphonphimok Prasat in the Grand Palace compound. Built in the reign of King Rama IV, this was used as a changing pavilion and also as a place to mount royal elephants and palanquins.

The Royal Elephant Stables, 1867

LUDOVIC HEBERT, Marquis of Beauvoir, spent a week in Bangkok in January 1867, during the reign of King Mongkut (Rama IV). One of the many remarkable things he saw in this brief stay, after watching the King enter the Grand Palace, was the royal elephant stables; and while some of his statistics may be doubtful, the visual impression is no doubt accurate.

"Not far from there are the royal stables, full, not of horses, but of elephants. We examined them minutely. Each animal has his shed of ten square yards, where he is fastened by one foot. We threw them small bunches of green corn; after having saluted us three times by raising their trunks to their full height, they shook our gifts to get off the dust, and swallowed them very delicately. Then we saw one ready armed for war; his great tusks were longer than a man, and a crocodile's skin was placed on his head to protect him from the blows of the enemy. A Siamese sergeant-major, wearing a helmet, was perched up on his seat, beneath the shade of a seven-storied umbrella, which is an emblem of royalty; and a quantity of lances, pikes, javelins, clubs, and tomahawks were arranged around him. The driver was seated behind, and with a sharp, childish voice guided the colossus of the animal kingdom. We chose to scale this living mountain, too, and feel the rocking motion of its trotting. And oh! how small everyone did look from the height, and how the swaying motion reminded us of a rolling sea! We saw twenty elephants huts in succession; I do not know exactly how many there are altogether. But it seems that when the king goes up the country, all the chiefs join him, accompanied by a squadron of elephants.... Even in this century there have been battles where six thousand could be counted in the two camps; and two-and-twenty years ago, when the Annamites invaded one of the provinces of Cambodia, the Siamese general, like a modern Samson, put them all to flight, by surprising them in the night with four hundred elephants to whose tails he had fastened flaming torches.

"But before us their performances were more peaceful; some of them disported themselves in perfect freedom in a great court, winking their cunning little eyes (the most cunning, it is said, in the animal kingdom), playing a thousand tricks, jumping clumsily, and taking care to avoid one another... The awkward movements of their unwieldly trunks made us shout with laughter, which seemed to hurt the feelings of the elephants and their ladies; I never should have expected them to be so touchy."

The rest of the tamed elephants were either sold on the local market or sent abroad, particularly to Indian states around the Bay of Bengal, where there was a continuing demand.

Mergui, a port now in Burma but then a Siamese possession, was a major center for such export trade. The elephants were brought by land down to Tenasserim, about halfway across the narrow southern peninsula, then placed in broad, flat-bottomed boats and floated down to Mergui, where they were embarked fourteen to twenty at a time on ships. On the voyage, which lasted between two and three weeks, each elephant had to be provided with at least seventy banana trees and plenty of fresh water for food, no easy task in a wooden 17th-century vessel.

There were occasional mishaps. In 1650, a sailor named John Struys accidentally spilled hot soup on one of the huge passengers, causing him to "roar and stamp, [so] that the ship tumbled and shaked again." For his error, Struys was tied to the mast and lashed "lustily with a rope's end," a punishment that was relatively moderate in view of the fact that the maddened elephant might well have brought down the ship along with all aboard.

Like King Chulalongkorn later, King Narai had the idea of offering elephants as royal gifts. During the elephant hunt he staged for the French embassy in 1685, he decided to send a small one to the Duke of Burgundy on the returning ship. "A half-hour later," the Abbé Choisy wrote, "he remembered His Royal Highness the Duke of Anjou and said he did not want to cause him to cry, and it was necessary to give him one too." The Abbé viewed this generosity with some alarm; each of the little animals, he observed, "weighs as much as a good half-dozen bulls; they will complicate things a lot." His prediction proved all too true. When the numerous other gifts from the King were loaded on the ship - more than 300 bales, according to a partial list - they proved more than it could carry, and at the last minute the elephants were removed, along with a number of chests.

By the mid-nineteenth century, elephants were no longer being used for war in Thailand, but throughout the country - and even to an extent in Bangkok, where some of the first roads were built along old elephant tracks - their strength and skills were still being put to many uses. King Mongkut (Rama IV) had this in mind when he wrote a letter to the American President James Buchanan on February 14, 1861, accompanying some

Above: Old photograph showing elephants in war regalia. (Courtesy of the National Archives)

presents sent aboard the *John Adams* commanded by a Captain Berrien:

"During the interview in reply from Captain Berrien to our inquiries of various particulars relating to America, he stated that on that continent there are no elephants. Elephants are regarded as the most remarkable of the large quadrupeds by the Americans so that if anyone has an elephant's tusk of large size, and will deposit it in any public place, people come by thousands crowding to see it, saying, it is a wonderful thing...

"Having heard this it has occurred to us that, if on the continent of America there should be several pairs of young male and female elephants turned loose in the forests where there was an abundance of water and grass in any region under the sun's declination both North and South, called by the English the Torrid Zone - and all were forbidden to molest them, to attempt to raise them would be well and if the climate there should prove favorable to the elephants, we are of the opinion that after a

while they will increase till there be large herds as there are here on the continent of Asia until the inhabitants of America will be able to catch them and tame and use them as beasts of burden making them of benefit to the country..."

The King concluded by saying that if the project was approved and a suitable vessel was provided, he would "procure young male and female elephants and forward them one or two pairs at a time." Perhaps to emphasize his point about the appeal of tusks, the King included among his presents an impressive pair.

By the time the letter arrived, conditions in the U.S. had changed rather drastically. Abraham Lincoln was president, and the Civil War was raging. Lincoln replied on February 3, 1862, thanking him for the generous offer but regretfully refusing it: "Our political jurisdiction... does not reach a latitude so low as to favor the multiplication of the elephant, and steam on land, as well as on water, has been our best and most efficient agent of transportation..."

Above: Carved elephant tusks, among the gifts presented by King Rama V for the Siam Exhibit in the Centennial Exposition, 1876. (Courtesy of The Smithsonian Institution)

A Northern Courtship

W.A. R. WOOD was probably the best loved and the most distinguished of the farang *community in Chiang Mai. Born near Liverpool in 1878, he entered the British consular service at an early age and arrived in Bangkok in 1896. His first upcountry posting was to Nan, after which he went to Chiang Rai and to various other places before coming to Chiang Mai in 1913. He remained there until his death in 1970 at the age of 91.*

The following account of his courtship of the girl he married is from De Mortuis: The Story of the Chiang Mai Foreign Cemetery *by R.W. WOOD (no relation). According to the author, "It may be taken with a great deal of salt but it is not greatly unfactual... Girls of 14 were certainly considered of marriageable age in those days, while a foreign suitor would naturally consider it more proper to wait.*

Baggage elephants were always knocking down people's houses and crops in search of fodder, and the accident of an elephant uniting young lovers is as easy as boy-meets-girl at the pony club."

"Once upon a time there was a poor young consul who lived in Nan. His only friend was an elephant, and often they would go for long walks together in the forest, arm-in-trunk, when the elephant would put their suitcases on his back and everything else including the kitchen stove (for he never forgot anything). The elephant was much older and wiser than the consul, and was a well-educated elephant, and would say things like 'nil desperandum' and 'pro bono publico' and 'handsome is as handsome does.' He was also quite musical.

"One day they came to Chiang Rai and camped near the house of a well-connected farmer. As they sat sipping their tea,

a beautiful girl (she was only 14 but really quite grown up) rode by astride a buffalo and went into the farmer's house. The consul jumped up and said, 'I love that girl, tomorrow we will go to the farmer and ask for her hand in marriage.' The elephant was so surprised he could only say 'caveat emptor,' which was a breach of best taste.

"So next day they went to the farmer and the consul said, 'I love your daughter to desperation. Let us become engaged and after two years I will come back and marry her.' But the farmer (who had done his homework) said, 'You are a poor man. You have no land and no house. Also you are a curious foreigner. Get your great red face out of here.' The little girl (who had been watching through the bamboo wall) said, 'You are unkind,' but the farmer replied, 'Unkind to a foreigner? Bah!' She said, 'I mean me,' and burst into tears.

"The consul and the elephant went back to Nan, where the consul was very sad and glum for two years, which also upset the elephant who said 'nil desperandum' and 'there's just as good fish in the sea, you know' and played trumpet voluntaries by Jeremiah Clark, though surprisingly none of them seemed to relieve his friend's melancholy. However, after two years the consul was ordered to Chiang Rai to open a new consulate there, and they set off again, the elephant deep in thought and saying nothing except (forgetting himself for once) 'You're a crafty young b—— to have swung Chiang Rai for yourself!'

"On arrival at Chiang Rai they again camped near the house of the well-connected farmer, and as they sat sipping their lemonade the elephant, still deep in thought, jumped up and said, 'Eureka! It is time for my luncheon. I see a patch of well-grown *euphorbia sinensis* beyond the farmer's house. I will go and sample it.' So off he went but when he got to the farmer's house he said, 'This path is too narrow, it should be widened pro bono publico.' So he sat upon the farmer's house and squashed it, and went to eat the *euphorbia sinensis*. The farmer was very angry and said, 'You have destroyed my house and my *euphorbia sinensis*. I am ruined and must be compensated.' The elephant raised his hat (it was a solar topi) with his trunk and said, 'Good afternoon, sir. I see you have indeed suffered some loss. Let us go to my friend the consul who I am sure will compensate you. And where is your charming daughter today?'

"Back they went to the consul who said, 'I see you have indeed suffered loss and must be compensated. I have come to live here for some years and must build myself a house and consulate. Why should I not build you too a fine new house? And (touching upon our last interview) where is your charming daughter today?' So they sat awhile and talked (the farmer's daughter had now joined them) until they were all truly compensated, and later on the consul and his bride went to the missionary (there is always a missionary where there are woeful pagans) who said, 'Tut! tut!' and 'Are you quite sure?', as it is always a slight shock when a true christian wishes to marry a woeful pagan. And so they were married, and as they had always been quite sure they lived happily ever after."

Opposite: Hand-colored wood-engraving; Paris, 1870. (Courtesy of Joerg Kohler)

When the elephant was used for transportation, as the great majority were, passengers generally sat in a howdah, a chair-like seat tied to the animal's back. These varied greatly in both comfort and workmanship. The simplest, used by ordinary people, were called *sapakhab* in Thai and consisted merely of a seat with raised sides and back and splayed legs, while those used by royalty, called *phra thiang praphasthong* or *phra tinang lakho,* were elaborate roofed pavilions made of rare woods and often highly decorated.

Claude Ceberet du Boullay, who came with Simon de la Loubère's mission to Ayutthaya in 1687, noted such class distinctions when he made the overland trip across the southern peninsula to Mergui on his way home. His own howdah, he reported, was "a gilded seat covered with a kind of dome serving as an umbrella, upheld by four columns, the whole well gilded and decorated with carpets and cushions with gold brocade... My elephant was followed by ten others, on each of which was a chair and a round covering like those on the barges of the nobles; some were of red lacquer and others black and gilded overall. The ten elephants were mounted by people in my party and followed by eighteen others with whole bamboo covers for my servants and liverymen."

Nicholas Gervaise noted that etiquette was involved in the use of howdahs at this time: "When a mandarin is mounted on an elephant in the presence of His Majesty he may not use a howdah but is obliged to crouch on the animal's neck, but when the King is not there he may use a howdah that can be adjusted to form a saddle, on which he can sit very comfortably. An elephant usually carries four people, two in the howdah, one on the hindquarters, and one on the neck. These last two are called conaques [mahouts], that is to say elephant-guides. They make them kneel and get up when their riders want to mount and dismount."

(Howdahs were far more spectacular in ancient times, if Marco Polo is to be believed. He wrote that Kublai Khan, riding out to war, "took his station in a large wooden castle, borne on the backs of four elephants... The castle contained many crossbow-men and archers and on the top of it was hoisted the imperial standard, adorned with representations of the sun and the moon." A European writer in India, however, doubts whether any such vast contraptions ever existed outside medieval imagination.)

Carl Bock, a Norwegian naturalist who visited northern Thailand toward the end of the 19th century, found that even in a "commodious" howdah, travel by elephant back was difficult at first:

Above: Old photograph showing howdahs. (Courtesy of National Archives)
Opposite: A royal howdah, or elephant seat, dating from the early Bangkok period. (National Museum, Bangkok)

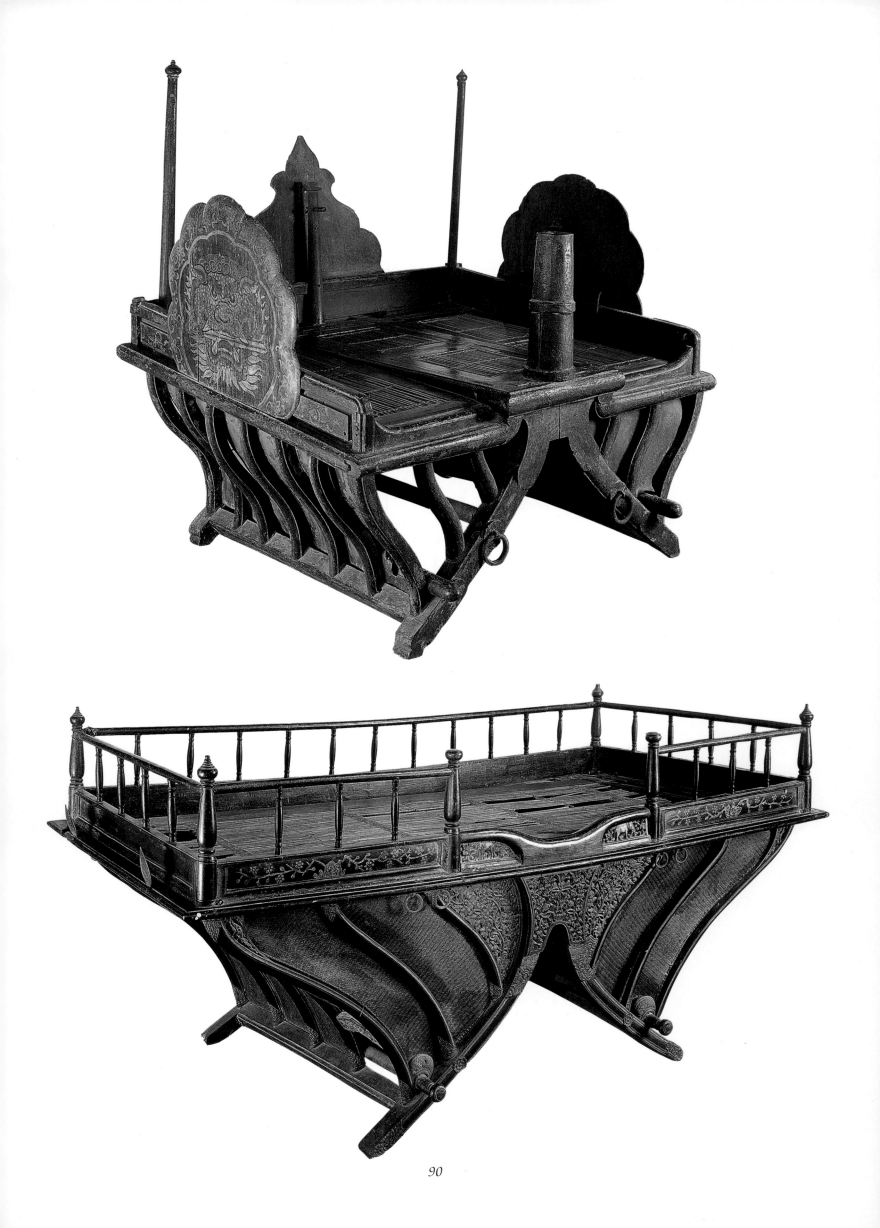

Clockwise from above: Howdah of early Bangkok period (National Museum, Bangkok);
howdah of former ruler of Nan. (National Museum, Nan); howdah in Bangkok style (Wang Chankasem Museum, Ayutthaya); war howdah,
the central pole being used for mounting a gun, from the turn of the century (Wang Chankasem Museum, Ayutthaya).

"The sensation is something like that of being rocked - not too gently, and with a circular movement - in a huge cradle. The pace is slow, and this mode of locomotion altogether tedious, though, when the country is open, there is an advantage to the fine view to be had from a height of ten to eleven feet or more from the ground."

(Bock suffered humiliation as well as tedium during his tour. Female elephants, though often easier to ride than males, were looked down upon locally as transports, and thus he protested when offered one. No male was available, though, and he had to accept, with the result that "the natives, in many out of the way places especially, offered me insults, and placed impediments in my way, which they would never have dared to do if I had ridden a *tusker*.")

Around the time Bock made his journey, elephants were much in demand in the far north. Treaties signed by King Mongkut with various European powers had led to a huge increase in trade, and one of the commodities most in demand was teak, available in abundance in forests of the region. Logging concessions were leased by the Thai government, mostly to foreigners - among those granted one was Louis T. Leonowens, son of the famous Anna - and systematic felling of the trees began.

Historically, the great teak boom was relatively brief - evidence that easily accessible forests were being exhausted was clear as early as 1890 - and the number of elephants employed in it was always small compared with those used for transporting goods and people; but popular books with titles like *Elephant Bill* and *Teak Wallah* gave the industry an allure far beyond the region, and while it lasted places like Chiang Mai and Lampang in northern Thailand prospered.

Elephants involved in the work were enrolled at the age of three to five in training schools. There they learned to get to know their mahouts and understand commands, many of these the same ones that had been employed for centuries, such as *song*, summoning the animal to lower its front legs and allow the mahout to climb up, and *how*, ordering it to stop; still others ordered it to get up, crouch down, pick up, and move around. Over the next five or six years, they were taught such tasks as lifting logs with their trunks and tusks, piling them up, and dragging selected logs through the thick, roadless forests to the nearest river. The logs thus collected were floated to an assembly point and tied into immense rafts for the long journey down to Bangkok's sawmills; by 1904, some 100,000 logs were arriving annually at Paknam Po, near Nakhon Sawan, the point where the Chao Phraya River begins and where they were graded and taxed.

Preceding spread: Detail of mural at Wat Sao Hin, Lamphun.
Above: Old photograph showing teak logging. (Courtesy of National Archives)

The better logging companies took good care of the elephants they employed for these tasks, giving them a holiday to roam in the forest during the hottest months of the year, inspecting them regularly for any sign of ill health, and providing them with adequate supplies of food and water. Others, however, overworked their animals so that many died when they were around fifty years old, instead of the normal seventy or eighty.

A healthy work elephant in its prime, capable of pulling a log of two tons or more and depositing smaller ones precisely where directed, was a valuable possession. W.A.R. Wood in his memoirs recalled one occasion when a man he knew, "who rather fancied himself as an expert," got cheated in a transaction for what appeared a handsome strong young specimen. "Being short-sighted, he failed to observe that it had been polished up with oil and varnish, and that the deeper cracks in its sides had been payed out with tow and plaster. He agreed to pay a good price, and went next day to the Siamese District Officer's Court to pay the money and have the transfer papers made out. But while the District Officer's clerk was writing out the transfer paper, the poor veteran elephant lay down outside and died of old age."

Teak production reached a height in 1931, when around thirteen million cubic feet were felled;

by the 1960s, the figure was half that and falling rapidly. The reasons were various. Most important, of course, was the failure to plant new trees and to control logging, but there were others like the clearing of forests for agriculture and the use of new, less expensive building materials. The importance of elephants also declined as roads were built deeper into the remaining forests and machines took over much of the heavy work. In the late 1980s, at least officially though perhaps not in fact, all logging in Thai forests was banned by the government.

With their use in war, transport, and most other work effectively ended, Thai elephants today face a precarious future. Reliable estimates place the number of remaining wild elephants at between 1,000 and 1,500, about 200 of them at Khao Yai National Park on the fringe of the northeastern plateau and most of the others in such wildlife sanctuaries as Huai Kha Khaeng and Thung Yai Naresuan. Domesticated elephants are believed to number between 3,500 and 4,000.

Various acts concerning the elephant have been passed by the Thai government. Under the Wild Elephant Act of 1921, one of the first of its kind in the world, all wild specimens were declared the property of the government, with the Ministry of Interior representing the crown. Hunting

Above: Teak logging in northern Thailand. (Courtesy of National Archives)
Following spread: Elephants working in the northern teak forests. (Private Collection)

The Karens

The largest number of elephant-keepers in Thailand today are Karen, member of a tribal group along hundreds of kilometers of the mountainous border with Burma, about whose relationship with their animals little has been written. Many observers say that they are more genuinely kind to their elephants than others, treating them as they would a horse or an ox. According to Richard

Lair, nearly every Karen boy begins to play with elephant calves from a very early age, with the result that most Karen elephants can be ridden by a large number of mahouts instead of the two-man, one-elephant pattern found elsewhere. Owning one of the animals brings great prestige, even conveying a special title; one survey found that Karens would rather spend money to acquire an elephant than on fields, better houses, or traditional festivals.

Unlike other keepers, Karens usually prefer cows and mahouts who ride them are not considered less verile than those who ride bulls. When a visitor asked one the reason for his

preference, he was told, "Cows can have babies!"

Karens have their own rituals for capturing and training elephants, though these seem to be fading among the younger men as life becomes more difficult for them due to constant fighting by rival forces in the area. Nevertheless, it is thought that many of the elephants being smuggled from Burma into Thailand were captured by members of the tribe and some may be involved in illegal logging. A number have brought their elephants to Thailand to escape the turmoil in Burma and offer rides to tourists in various parts of the north, while still others, who have no animals of their own, work as mahouts in shows around Mae Hong Sorn and Chiang Mai.

The Karen population is believed to be around 2.5 million; some 200,000 live in northern Thailand and another 100,000 further south along the border with Burma.

Above: Karens of the Le Tong Khu village in Tak displaying one of their prized heirlooms, a pair of intricately carved elephant tusks.
Left: The Karens are the only hilltribe that utilizes elephants.

the animals as sport was strictly forbidden by the act, and all elephants with certain characteristics regarded as "auspicious" were to be presented to the King. The Draught Animal Act of 1939 specifically classified the domesticated elephant as a draft animal (*sat phahana*), such as horses, water buffaloes, and cows, and required them to be registered as such in the eighth year of age; the act clearly considered elephants to be private property, though it made no provision for their treatment by owners. The Wildlife Protection Act of 1992 was aimed at preserving wild specimens, specifically excluding registered draft animals covered by the 1939 act, but this has aroused considerable controversy among conservationists over whether domesticated elephants are, or should be, included in its provisions.

Thanks to an expanding population and the consequent need for more land for farming, the wild elephant's domain is rapidly shrinking, and only constant efforts by forestry and environmental groups can preserve even the limited territory still available; newspaper reports in 1997-8 of elephants being killed by farmers whose crops they were destroying suggest that this problem is far from being resolved. Domesticated elephants present a different kind of problem, in a way even more complex. Here, on the one hand, is a treasured symbol of the nation, part of a rich cultural legacy going back a thousand years and enshrined in both art and legend. At the same time, it is a highly visible creature, very much alive, weighing up to six tons and requiring an immense amount of food every single day of its long life; moreover, it is one that elicits strong, deeply-rooted human emotions. How can these be reconciled? How can the symbol remain not merely a quaint figure in a mural painting or a tempting shape for woodcarvers but also a living animal with some role in daily life?

Various answers have been sought. The Elephant Roundup, an annual event staged in Surin Province by the Tourism Authority of Thailand, brings a hundred or more of the animals together for a popular demonstration of their skills and helps meet some of the expenses of their upkeep. Other elephants perform in shows staged at various resorts or carry tourists for a "jungle ride" through patches of remaining forest. Despite a recent law forbidding them, some mahouts from Surin also bring their animals to the traffic-clogged streets of Bangkok, earning money not only from tourists delighted by such an anachronistic sight but also from Thais who hope to earn good luck by walking under an elephant. Assorted groups, too, have been formed by which domesticated elephants can be "adopted" or otherwise supported through public donations.

But the essential question remains, and the ultimate future of the Thai elephant depends on whether long-term solutions can be discovered.

Preceding spread: Kui mahouts in the northeast of Thailand.
Above: Thai elephants earning their keep at the Thai Elephant Conservation Center.
Following spread: Tourists in front of Wat Phra Si Sanphet in Ayutthaya.

The Legend of Phra Mau Thao
By Peter Cuasay

Phra Mau Thao tales recount heroic experiences of ancient Kui hunters to teach cooperation and other survival lessons. This social learning celebrated in story until the stories are so old and familiar they join in the silence of special objects or everyday habits, is also crystallized in the customs of the Kui people. The Kui once roamed freely in the 'Emerald Triangle' area at the borders of Thailand, Cambodia, and Laos. They speak a Katuic branch of Mon-Khmer older than Ayutthaya, Angkor, and other kingdoms which prized their skills in working with elephants, iron, and silk.

The following story is the central Phra Mau Thao myth, revealing the Kui insight that knowledge is inseparable from responsibility, that violence at the origins of civilization must be balanced by wisdom and restraint.

Long ago, there were three great and ancient masters of hunting: Phra Mau Thao, Phra Wet Sindhon, and Phra Phram Chettabot. They roamed as friends, for what cannot be done by one man can be done by his friend; by joining together they can go far and reach wisdom. Once they traveled until they heard that people feared gigantic Phithikhot, lord and father of the elephant herd, who was able to speak the language of men, for in those times elephants could talk. Phra Mau Thao, Phra Wet Sindhon, and Phra Phram Chettabot resolved to set out and seek Phithikhot.

One day, they at last saw an enormous, magnificent elephant emerge to ask them, "Why have you come?" Phra Mau Thao answered "We come to see elephants, especially one named Phithikhot for we have heard he is a marvelous beast."

The elephant asked, "Have you come as hunters, come to kill?"

"No," replied Phra Mau Thao, "we just came to look. See, we have no weapons or equipment." He was lying to the elephant, for they had hidden their hunting gear.

"Look then," announced the elephant, "I am Phithikhot, the elephant you seek. What do you want to see?"

Phra Mau Thao persuaded the elephant to show off. He brought vines to bind the elephant, who broke them all to show his strength. The three friends would challenge Phithikhot to break down trees. Every tree they pointed out, he could ram until it fell. At last, Phra Mau Thao said, "Here is one vine you have not tried. I think you cannot break it. Are you ready to let me tie you with one strand of this vine?"

Phithikhot was flush with victories, and let them tie his hind leg. The elephant did not know Phra Mau Thao had deceived him. The 'vine' was really buffalo hide braided into a *pakam* or lasso. Phithikhot

Opposite: Stone lintel at Prasat Ban Phluang near Surin depicting Indra on his mount Erawan.
Above: Kui elders in traditional ceremonial garment. (Royal Elephant National Museum)
Following page: Bronze statue of the Supreme Master of the Mahouts. (Royal Elephant National Museum)

strained but the 'vine' held him tight. He struggled with all his power, but the *pakam* did not break. However he roared and battered, he could not escape the lasso.

Phra Mau Thao eventually tamed Phithikhot, who had to accept his orders and let men ride on his neck. Before returning to the village of men, Phra Mau Thao cut out Phithikhot's tongue so that the beast could make only dumb sounds just like a man whose tongue has been chopped out. Phra Mau Thao's leadership enabled the men of olden times to capture all the talking elephants. Phithikhot's herd is no more, but even today elephants seem as if they could speak, but sound like their tongues were cut out.

Many years passed, the three friends dared many journeys, and Phra Mau Thao's glory was great. But his happiest moment came with his first and only child. His wife (whose name has been forgotten) gave birth to a son named Kong. Following the custom then, the firstborn male of a Phra Mau Thao, or highest master hunter, would inherit his father's title.

But in Kong's past life, he was an elephant calf. He could remember his past life, his elephant mother, and how he had been separated from her when captured by a hunter or Mau. In Kong's past life, he became a domesticated elephant but died young from the grief of losing his mother.

One day, Phra Mau Thao decided to bring Kong into the forest as his Ma, the apprentice who rides on the hindquarters of the elephant and obeys the Mau seated on the elephant's neck. Phra Mau Thao also invited his wife into the forest. But they left alone without telling anybody that they were beginning a hunt. Perhaps Phra Mau Thao wanted to give his son special individual training in secret. Perhaps Phra Mau Thao loved his son so much that he was anxious that Kong's first hunting experience be regarded as successful. So breaking with custom, his family set out alone secretly, all riding on the same elephant.

As soon as he saw signs of a wild elephant, Phra Mau Thao let his wife go down to stay at the campsite. He used his powerful spells to make a sacred boundary to protect his wife from harm. Then taking Kong he set off in the tracks of the wild elephant.

When they sighted elephants, Kong impetuously urged his father, "Catch the mother elephant because if you do you will get the children." Phra Mao Thao reproved Kong, because his custom was only to capture the elephant calf. Then he steered his chaser elephant after the calf so he could shoot a loop of *pakam* leather around its hind leg. Seeing his father about to lasso the calf, Kong was suddenly stricken with sorrow, and could do nothing but look at the mother elephant....and then he recognized that she was his own mother in his past life!

Before Phra Mau Thao took his shot to catch the calf, Kong jumped on the mother's back and away they fled into the big forest. Phra Mau Thao was so shocked to see Kong shoot through the air to land on the back of the wild mother elephant that for the first time in his life he failed to make a capture. Rapidly he turned the chaser elephant and tore after the wild elephant mother, following Kong into the woods.

"Kong ooy!" called Phra Mau Thao. And Kong answered "Kuk!" so his father could follow the sound. They called and shouted over and over, "Kong ooy....Kuk! Kong ooy...Kuk!" until the echoes rang fainter and fainter in the gathering darkness of the branches. In the end, he came to the thick of the jungle and found no tracks or traces. Then Phra Mau Thao knew he had lost his only son. No sign of him was ever seen again.

Phra Mao Thao turned back to camp to tell his wife. When he arrived at the place, he saw blood everywhere, his wife's things scattered. The scene told the tale: A tiger had ambushed the woman, so she fled for the safety of the sacred circle. When the tiger pounced and devoured her, she had gotten only part of her hand into the boundary protected by Phra Mau Thao's spell. The mutilated hand, just three fingers, was the only remnant that survived. Phra Mau Thao tied his wife's hand to the lasso and shaken, turned homeward.

Phra Mau Thao had lost everything, his one son was gone, his wife was dead. He told the elephant hunters of his village: "I ask that all of you use this piece on the end of the lance, for it can hold the *pakam* lasso like the fingers of a hand, and call this piece *khaen nang*, meaning my wife's hand. Whenever you go into the forest, I say: speak of my son Kong. He is now the lord of wild elephants. When hunting or training elephants, call on Kong."

He told Phra Khru Pakam: "Never again will I hunt, verily do I renounce this title of Phra Mau Thao." So Phra Khru Pakam ordered the Kui elephant men to learn from the experiences of Phra Mau Thao. He ordered new laws:

Father may not take son to be Mau and Ma together on the hunt.

Husband may not bring wife into forest.

A Mau who has captured a wild elephant may not ride that elephant on the hunt.

Phra Khru Pakam said these rules must be followed strictly, passed down the generations as the customary law of the elephant hunt. In time, the system of rules, ranks, and taboos became extensive, but presiding over all was Phra Khru Pakam, invoked constantly in the rituals of Kui elephant men. Beyond that lies the title of Phra Mau Thao, which has been empty since the renunciation, like a king who does not rule, like a hero who now lives only as a word. The myth of the mutilated hand of Phra Mau Thao's wife became a symbol of women's sacrifice; a woman's true love is like a sacred *pakam* hunting lasso: nothing can break it. And although Phra Mau Thao's son Kong vanished in the forest to become the Lord of Wild Elephants, others in the Emerald Triangle tell stories of a nameless orphan who tended buffaloes to earn his keep. Only this 'uncivilized' youth was able to bring back the three-headed elephant to aid the fight of a kingdom in need.

Sources: Kamluang Peud Phao Saendi, Mau Sadiang Kae Miw Salangam, Phra Ajarn Han Panyatharo.

Peter Cuasay is a doctoral candidate in anthropology at the University of Washington. He is studying the relationship between Kui culture in the nations of Thailand, Cambodia, and Laos.

The White Elephant

In 1858, returning to Thailand after a successful diplomatic mission to London, the Thai delegates submitted a report on an audience granted by Queen Victoria. "One cannot help but be struck with the aspect of the august Queen of England," they wrote, "or fail to observe that she must be of pure descent from a race of godly and warlike kings and rulers of the earth, in that her eyes, complexion, and above all her bearing, are those of a beautiful and majestic white elephant."

To outsiders, the description might seem whimsical. To others, however, among them the Thai king to whom the report was addressed, it amounted to praise of the very highest order; for no other animal has ever been accorded such enormous respect as the white elephant.

It is perhaps as well to state right away that the name is highly misleading, at least to Western readers. "There has never been such a thing as a white elephant," W.A.R. Wood once wrote, "and no Siamese ever speaks of such a creature. The animals which are venerated by old-fashioned Siamese, and some of which are kept in the royal palace as appurtenances of royalty, are in fact albinos, and are called by the Siamese *Chang Pheuak*, which simply means 'Albino Elephants.' Albino buffaloes are very common, and they are also called *pheuak*; the same word is used for human albinos."

Wood thinks the English term arose because of the white elephant that once appeared on the Thai flag and that became closely identified with the kingdom; this, however, seems unlikely in view of the fact that it was used long before the flag in question existed. Moreover, although *chang pheuak* is used by many Thai writers, translating it simply as 'albino elephant' is misleading. Many of the animals so designated are not true albinos but rather what specialized manuals on the subject call *chang samkhan*, 'important' or 'illustrious' elephants, fulfilling a complex set of requirements that include many features besides color. In any event, white or not, the rare animal has exerted a potent fascination for foreign visitors, especially those who recorded their experiences in popular books. Often they were disappointed, or, perhaps with tongue in cheek, professed themselves to be. "Were I to describe him as white," wrote Carl Bock, who saw one belonging to King Chulalongkorn in 1883, "I should lay

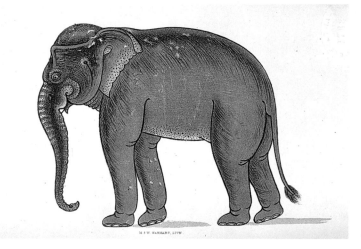

Preceding spread: Mural from Wat Phra Kaew Wang Na showing a battle between the princes of Chiang Mai & Chiang Rai in 1407. *Opposite:* White elephant in mother-of-pearl inlay, one of the 108 auspicious signs of the Buddha that adorn the soles of the feet on the Reclining Buddha at Wat Po. *Above:* Lithograph from Sir John Bowring's *Kingdom & People of Siam*; London, 1857 (Courtesy of Joerg Kohler)

myself open to the charge of color-blindness; but he was quite an albino, the whole body being of a pale reddish-brown color, with a few real white hairs on the back. The iris of the eye, the color of which is held to be

and Indo-China. (There is also a record of white elephants being sent overland in 1103 AD to Yunnan from what is today Malaysia.) Possession of such an auspicious animal was one of the attributes

a good test of an albino, was a pale Naples yellow. He looked peaceful enough, led, not ridden, by his carnac [mahout], and his quiet bearing was in great contrast with the excitement all around, as if he felt the importance of his position."

High expectations on the part of innocent spectators may account for why one specimen, allegedly acquired in Burma for a small fortune by the showman P.T. Barnum, proved disappointing as an attraction in Europe and America. It also proved difficult to dispose of, which, according to one source, gave rise to the expression "white elephant" for "a possession that is valuable but too burdensome to keep." This explanation, though it sounds doubtful, is certainly more persuasive than the more common one claiming that kings once gave white elephants to unpopular courtiers in order to ruin them financially. Instead, kings measured their greatness by the number of white elephants that came into the royal stables and, indeed, fought disastrous wars to keep them.

Reverence for the white elephant goes far back in Asian culture, originating in India but reaching a peak in Burma, Thailand,

of the Universal King, as explained in the *Traibhumikatha*, or *Three Planes of Existence*, one of the earliest texts translated into Thai and it figured in Buddhist belief as well. The Lord Buddha is said to have appeared to his mother, Queen Sirimahamaya, in the shape of a white elephant just before his birth. H. Quaritch Wales, in *Siamese State Ceremonies*, recounts this miraculous event as follows:

"Then the future Buddha, who had become a superb white elephant, and was wandering on the Golden Hill, not far from there, descended thence, and ascending the Silver Hill, approached her from the North. Holding in his silvery trunk a white lotus flower, and uttering a far-reaching cry, he entered the golden mansion, and thrice doing obeisance to his mother's couch, he gently struck her right side, and seemed to enter her womb."

The last and most popular of the Jataka stories, about the Buddha's previous lives, tells of how when Prince Vessantara was a baby a young white elephant was brought to the royal stables and thus the two grew up together; though the animal is much beloved by his people because of its power

Above: Drawing in a book by Carl Bock of a white elephant from the reign of King Rama V. (Courtesy of Joerg Kohler)
Opposite: The Buddha's mother dreams of a white elephant; mural at Phra Thinang Phutthaisawan, National Museum, Bangkok.

to bring rain, the prince shows his generosity by giving the noble animal to a neighboring kingdom suffering from drought. This is, incidentally, the only example in Asian literature of a white elephant being given freely away, and the point is to demonstrate extraordinary virtue.

The first mention of a white elephant in Thai history appears in the famous inscription of King Ramkamhaeng of Sukhothai already cited in the previous chapter. Association of the animal with royal wealth and power was well established by 1545 when Fernao Mendes Pinto, a Portuguese adventurer, visited the next capital of Ayutthaya and saw one of the palace specimens being taken to bathe in the river: "He was shaded from the sun by twenty-four servants carrying white parasols. His guard numbered three thousand men. It was like a procession on a day of festival. Before and behind went about thirty lords on elephants. He had a chain of beaten gold on his back and thick silver chains girding him like belts. Round his neck were more silver chains. They told me that on feast days he wore gold chains, but silver chains when he was going to his bath. In his trunk he carried a golden globe, of about twice the size of a man's head, that seemed to be a cosmographical sphere. They had a stage for him to stand on at the water's edge. I did not see the ceremonies with which they washed him, but I am told they were very many. The streets through which he passed were beflagged and decorated like in Portugal for the big bull-fights or royal feasts."

King Mahachakrapat was ruler of Ayutthaya at the time, and the elephant Pinto saw was presumably one of an unusual number of albinos found during his reign, leading him to be known as "Lord of the White Elephants"; the most prized, a specimen seven feet tall, was given various noble titles, among them "the gem of the sky," "the glory of the land," and "the radiance of the world." Such good fortune, however, also had its disadvantages. In particular, it aroused the envy of the Burmese King Bayinnaung, who asked for two of the elephants as a sign of cordial relations. According to historian Rong Syamananda, the request was seriously considered by a council of princes and high officials; one conciliatory faction was in favor of granting it to preserve peace while another was strongly opposed. King Mahachakrapat agreed with the latter - an unfortunate choice, as it turned out, since Ayutthaya not only lost the war that ensued but also four instead of only two of its white elephants. The auspicious animals ended up in Pegu, where Ralph Fitch, the

Above: Painting on glass; early twentieth century. (Collection of Professor Arun Chaiseri)
Opposite: Painting on cloth depicting an episode from the Vessantara Jataka;
Prince Vessantara demonstrates his charitable nature by giving away a precious rain-making
white elephant. (Courtesy of Jim Thompson Foundation)

first Englishman to visit Burma, saw them in 1585 and described their loving treatment in much the same way as Pinto.

(Burma's last white elephant was treated far less grandly. A year after Mandalay fell to the British in 1885, it, along with other royal treasures, was taken down the Irrawaddy in a steamboat to Rangoon. There it was placed in the Zoological Gardens in a special pavilion. After its death in 1910, its tusks were taken to Ireland and presented to the National Museum in Dublin; they were returned by request of the Burmese Government in 1964.)

The specific physical characteristics of a *chang pheuak* had long been codified by this time. As recorded in early Bangkok, along with many other traditions of Ayutthaya, these were complex and required certification by an expert attached to the royal court. Eleven specific distinguising marks are cited in one account:

1. A white or pinkish color around the cornea of the eyes;
2. The roof of the mouth pink and unridged;
3. A characteristic skin fold around the shoulders;
4. The skin surrounding the tusks the same color as under the shoulders;
5. White or pink genitals;
6. White or pink toenails;
7. Light brown hair that is transparent when held up to light;
8. Cuticles that are lighter than the surrounding skin;
9. Orifice of the musk gland in the head a different color from that of ordinary elephants;
10. Two body hairs growing out of one follicle

11. An overall body color of chestnut gray.

To these, an illustrated manuscript called *The Book on Elephant Science*, produced in the early 19th century, adds that the elephant should be fragrant smelling and, when asleep, always facing an auspicious direction, should not snore loudly but emit a sound similar to that of Thai classical music. (Other accounts claim that the normal call of a white elephant should resemble the sound made by blowing into a sacred conch shell, an essential object in various Hindu and Brahmin ceremonies that are a part of Thai ritual.)

There are in fact three classes of white elephant, each with subdivisions. Even if a specimen fails to qualify for the very highest rank it is still regarded as auspicious and given special treatment.

By ancient custom, and by law since the Elephant Maintenance Act of 1921, anyone finding an elephant with these characteristics must offer it to the King and will be compensated if it is accepted by the experts. Two such animals were discovered during the reign of King Rama I, who founded the present Chakri Dynasty and established Bangkok as the capital. One, it is said, though belonging to the third rank, was nevertheless deemed desirable and its owner was ordered to present it to the monarch. Unhappy at losing the animal, the owner cut off its tail to reduce its value, an act that incurred royal displeasure and cost the owner the usual reward given in such circumstances. Subsequently, however, a statue commemorating the elephant was placed in the Temple of the Emerald Buddha.

Opposite: Murals of one of the scripture repositories at Wat Po are a treatise on different kinds of auspicious elephants.

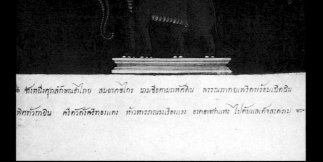

es from an early 19th century manuscript. Various kinds of auspicious elephants are shown on this page, while opposite are ones with undesirable features that include scaly, smelly skin, a ridged back, and short front legs . (Courtesy of National Library)

ฯ หนึ่งชื่อแยกเรียวกระ ฯ สิการกายา เล่นกลกลมกดทั่วกน ฯ ควานกกมันงาม

ยืนเหมนเหลืงตน แสงกระลาเหมนเรียว พังพลายทรไทยทับเรียว เหมือนกันคุรเถียว

อย่าเถาเลียงไว้อีก ฯ

ฯ ทังซ้ายสินมิถยโถษา ฯ สิกลลกิกรณ เหลืงนันยอมิสิงกิ ฯ เการิจกรเกกิ กล้าขน

กิ้ จึงเกเลเกนิกนุไป ยังซิริอรมพละนุกได้ ฯ ญิญูฐานในไกร ปุกงยเกเปนตการ

ว่าท้ำใหญ่สูงประมาณ ฯ รุปอรรินทน ประเท่าผิงพร้นิท ฯ นุกกเรียวที่สุดแกนแกน

หนังหาราดา แกรนประมณเสิบหนึ่ง ฯ เรียงพัดลเหมนมเรียงริม ฯ เกรียกเกรียก

ฯ หนึ่งชื่อราฆกรรษ ฯ สิการลกรรณ หลังหยักกเกกกงทกด ฯ ถึงตรทังท้ายปกกฎ

ทางเรินกกทด ฯ ภกามกิกลลที่ไว้ ฯ

ฯ ตังหนิ้ชิ่งศัคธรเษิ ฯ ท้ำหนักหัดกิ ฯ ถกว่าท้ำวหลังกุมพด กุตุมกัณฑ์กายกกล กัมแต

วกก หนึ่งเยิงข่างท้ำวาง เหรียบมิเสมรขินกอน ท้ำงยู่กอน ฯ ถึงงามเยิิงเกิมใน

ลิน ท้ำวทงสินันใจวกัน แลงกกรกกา แนบวงลงไปแลท หลังกุมเรียงแท่ท้ำยม

Customs Concerning the Sacred White Elephant

The following is compiled from Chang Thai *(Thai Elephants) by Professor Suthilak Ambhanwong, published by Matichon Press, September, 1994. The author lectures at Chulalongkorn University.*

During the reign of Rama VI, a bill for the preservation of wild elephants was passed in 1921. It specified that wild elephants were crown property and permission had to be obtained before they could be captured for use. The act was meant to protect wild elephants and preserve the species.

The act mentions elephants with special characteristics. According to article 4, these are of three categories:

(1) *Chang Samkhan,* or illustrious elephant, which is characterized by seven features - white eyes, white palate, white nails, white hair, white or clay-pot-color (reddish brown) skin, white tail hair, white or clay-pot-color testicles.

(2) *Chang Si-palad,* or strange-colored elephant, which possesses any of the illustrious elephant's seven features.

(3) *Chang Niam,* or short-tusked elephant, which is marked by three features - black skin, black nails, tusks shaped like banana flowers.

Article 32 of this act says that anyone who comes into possession of an illustrious elephant, a strange-colored elephant, or a short-tusked elephant and sets it free or keeps it in hiding commits a serious crime. He will be imprisoned for a maximum of one year or fined up to 500 baht. The elephant will be confiscated.

It can be seen that in this act there is no mention of the *Chang Pheuak,* the usual translation of 'white elephant.' Instead, there are three categories of white or illustrious elephants as mentioned above. It is regarded as an auspicious omen if a king comes into possession of several of these, meaning the country will enjoy peace and prosperity.

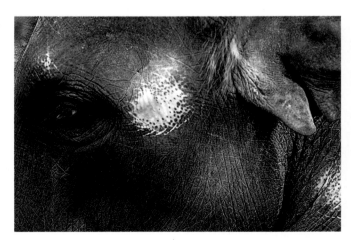

When an official learns that a white elephant has been born in a district, he will report to the king. An expert on elephant characteristics will be sent to verify the report. Besides the features specified in the manual on elephant characteristics, other favorable attributes have to be taken into consideration as well. For example, an elephant whose snoring is like the blowing of a conch shell is auspicious, while one that snores like a crying baby is merely lucky; such an animal as the latter, despite all its favorable features, will not be enrolled for celebration.

When the elephant in question has all the features and attributes characteristic of an auspicious elephant, the inspector will report to the king. The latter will order a proper ceremony, either at the place where the elephant is located or in Bangkok. If the royal ceremony is to be performed in Bangkok, a celebration will be held in the province where the elephant was captured prior to bringing it to Bangkok, and celebrations will be held in each of the provinces the elephant passes through or stops over in.

Examination of White Elephants

When there is a report that a white elephant has been found in a jungle or any location, the Royal Household Bureau will send out an expert to examine the features that mark it as a white elephant. There are eleven in all.

According to the manual on white elephants, the following features are to be examined - the hair, tail, eyes, nails, testicles, opening at the end of the trunk, pores, palate, flesh at the tusk base, and flesh under the nail. If these are of the auspicious color like that of the body, the most important feature, the animal passes the test. In the course of the examination, if the elephant has more than half of the required features, the inspector can conclude that it is an illustrious elephant without going over all the eleven features.

The examination will start with the color of

the body. In the case of a baby elephant, the body color is hard to determine. A common practice is to dissolve three or four kilos of ripe tamarind in water and apply the solution on the whole body, leave it overnight, and wash it off the next morning. The true color of the body can then be seen. Since elephants have body odor, detergent is not to be used as it will mask the real body odor.

The next step is to examine the hair, which means the hair on the ears, on the trunk, on the back, etc. Moreover, one can identify various kinds of elephants from their pores. Those of the highly desired Brahmapong family have two, three, four, or more hairs to a pore. Elephants of the other three families have only one hair in a pore. Besides, an elephant of the Brahmapong family has eight translucent hair follicles in one pore. If the follicles are joined in pairs, the animal is most likely to belong to the Brahmapong family.

Top-quality hair must be translucent, looking like glass. The second best is honey-colored and also translucent. Bad hair is that which is dull and opaque or curved sightly at the ends.

Also on the checklist of elephant character-istics are perfect ears and tail. The ears should not be torn or flayed; if they are, the elephant is of poor quality. A good tail must have hair on it; a hairless tail means the animal is not good. There are three types of tail - short, medium (long enough to wear an adornment with the tip showing), and long (meaning that the tip of the tail trails the ground).

Elephant eyes are difficult to examine. The palate and testicles, however, do not present much of a problem. As for nails, they are of two kinds, fibrous and shell-like.

Another spot to be examined is the fold in the foreleg area to see the color of the tender flesh there. The back has to be examined to determine the real color of the skin. The next step is to look at the color of the skin that covers the nails. The part that is easiest to inspect is the trunk. The end of its back shows the true color most clearly.

If the elephant fits the description of a white elephant, the Royal Household Bureau will be notified and the king will be informed. A royal celebration of the elephant will be held later.

Opposite: Marking on a white elephant. *Below:* Illustration showing deities that embody the various anatomical parts of an elephant.

Royal Ceremony to Mark the Registration of a White Elephant

The Royal ceremony in honor of an illustrious elephant can be considered an expression of gratitude to benefactors. The Thais are a people who feel indebted to whatever promotes the peace and happiness of the country, be it living or non-living, an animal, a human, or an object. The elephant has been of great use to the Thais in time of peace and war since ancient times. It can be considered a great benefactor of the people and the country.

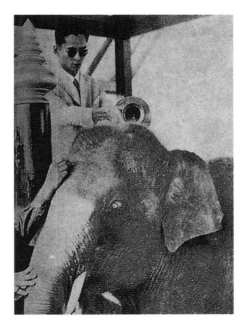

Such a practice is an indication of the spiritual development of a people.

Before the royal ceremony marking the registration of an illustrious elephant, the rite of tethering the animal is performed. The purpose of this rite is to apologize to the beast on which will later be bestowed an honor that is the equivalent of a prince. In the rite, the elephant will be tied to a stake to familiarize it with the rope and the corral and taught to stand tethered on a platform for a long time. The purpose is to get it accustomed to the new life and not be restless in front of the king on the day of the celebration.

The tethering ceremony consists of Buddhist and Brahmin rites. There are offerings of various kinds. An image of Ganesha, the god of the elephant, is also brought to the ceremonial site to bless the occasion. All the participants have to wear white costumes and make obeisance to the elephant because a white elephant has the same status as a prince of royal blood.

The registration ceremony begins with the king walking up to the platform where the elephant is tethered and pouring lustral water from a gourd and a royal conch shell on its head. He then steps down and stands in front of the elephant. Next he feeds the elephant three sections of red sugar cane, on which a Brahmin has inscribed its name. Afterwards the king gives a gold plate bearing the elephant's name and decorative trappings to the chief elephant trainer to put on the elephant. Finally he returns to his seat and the program arranged by the Royal Household Bureau proceeds. The main item is the recitation by a Brahmin of a poem pacifying the elephant, while an official rotates the handle of a small, two-faced drum and musicians from the Fine Arts Department play three-stringed fiddles to calm the animal.

The following day is the celebration. The king comes in the morning, and an official of the Elephant Department brings the elephant to bathe at a pavilion with all the paraphernalia indicating rank - a conch shell, a trumpet, and a kind of Javanese drum - playing in full honor. Then the elephant is towelled dry and led to preside behind a table with food for monks. The head of the Elephant Department and his assistant place food in the alms bowls of thirty monks on behalf of the elephant. After that both of them make obeisance to him as a way of reporting that they have completed their assignment. The elephant is then led to the platform and arrayed with all the trappings. The last item in the program comes when Brahmins and other participants pass from hand to hand lighted tapers, fixed in lenticular holders, around the elephant and fan the smoke towards him three times. This light-waving rite is intended to ward off evil influences.

Above: His Majesty King Bhumibol Adulyadej pouring lustral water on a white elephant in 1959. (Courtesy of Royal Household Bureau)

Four white elephants were recorded in King Rama II's reign. George Finlayson, who travelled with John Crawfurd on a mission to Thailand and Cochin-China in 1821-22, was taken on a tour of the king's palace and saw five of them in the royal stables, one presumably being from the former reign.

This number, he thought, suggested "that this variety is far less rare than we are accustomed to believe, at least, that is so in the further peninsula of India. It has, however, seldom happened that so many have been collected at one period, and the present is regarded as auspicious in consequence of an event so unexpected, and so much desired. A white elephant is still reckoned as beyond all value, every effort is made to take them when they are by chance discovered, and the subjects of the King can perform no more gratifying service than that of securing them." Finlayson adds, like so many other foreigners who actually saw one of the animals, "The appelation white, as applied to the elephants, must be received with some degree of limitation."

F.A. Neal, who lived in Bangkok toward the end of King Rama III's reign, proved an exception to this generally skeptical view. Of one of the two he was shown, he wrote, "I have never before seen as large an elephant; his skin was as smooth and spotless and white as the driven snow, with the exception of a large scarlet rim round the eyes. The brute was too dignified and accustomed to homage to pay the slightest attention to the intrusion of such unpresuming visitors as ourselves, but went on calmly helping himself to leaves and branches from the mighty piles that were heaped up before him."

King Mongkut (Rama IV) was perhaps the most advanced and liberal-minded of the early Chakri rulers. As a monk before he came to the throne, he sought to rid Buddhism of the superstitions that had become deeply ingrained in it; as king, he opened the country to trade with the West, became an expert astronomer, and sought to modernize his kingdom in countless ways. Yet he regarded white elephants with all the awe and reverence of his ancestors, as he made

Above: Lao silk with elephant motif. (Private Collection.)

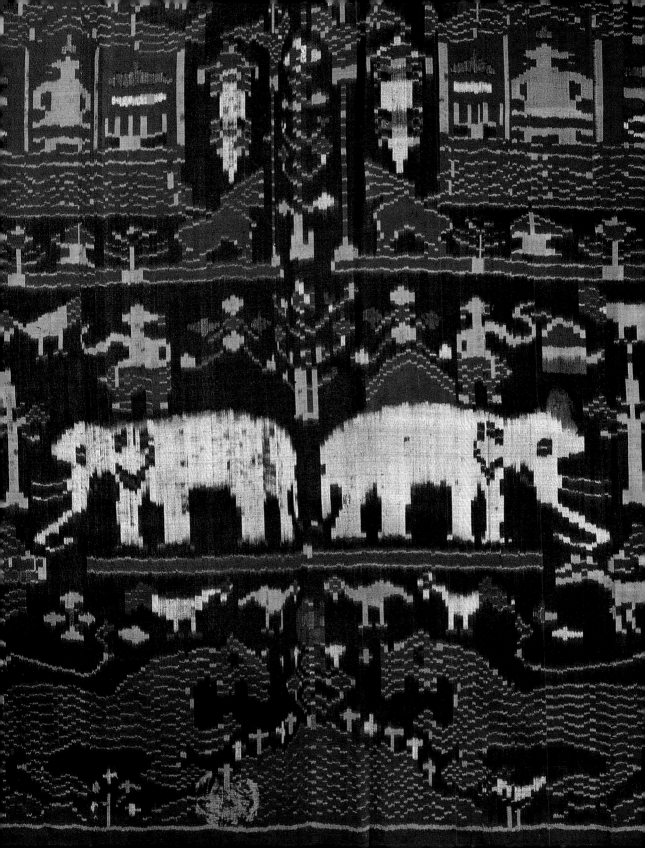

clear to Sir John Bowring, who came in 1855 to negotiate treaties.

"When a tributary king, or governor of a province, has captured a white elephant," Bowring wrote in his account of the mission, "he is directed to open a road through the forest for the comfortable transit of the sacred animal; and when he reaches the Meinam [i.e. the Chao Phraya River], he is received on a magnificent raft, with a chintz canopy, and garlanded with flowers. He occupies the center of the raft, and is pampered with cakes and sugar. A noble of high rank, sometimes a prince of royal blood (and on the last occasion both the First and Second Kings), accompanied by a great concourse of barges, with music and bands of musicians, go forth to welcome his arrival. Every barge has a rope attached to the raft, and perpetual shouts of joy attend the progress of the white elephant to the capital, where, on his arrival, he is met by the great dignitaries of the State, and by the Monarch himself, who gives the honored visitor some sonorous name, and confers on him the rank of nobility. He is conducted to a palace which is prepared

for him, where a numerous court awaits him, and a number of officers and slaves are appointed to administer to his wants in vessels of gold and silver."

This description was based on the festivities that greeted a female white elephant found in the previous year. In December, 1854, when plans for Bowring's visit were being made, the King wrote in his distinctive English warning of possible interruptions in his schedule as a result: "She is said to be in the same manner or kind of that one of my royal grandfather, and those three of my esteemed royal father... The she Elephant will be brought from hence where it was apprehended on the present month, and will be arrived at old capital 'Ayudhia' on next month, in which time I will be absent from home... about half a month more to welcome the white animal according to the former custom upon the reigns of my royal grandfather and late father, when their whitest elephants arrived."

Though Bowring missed the arrival ceremony, he was taken to see the elephant by one of the royal princes after an audience with the King. "Her color is really a light ma-

hogany," he wrote, "the eye that of an albino; but the animal appeared in perfect health, and occupied the center of a large apartment, in one part of which, in an elevated position, was a golden chair for the King... The elephant has a number of attendants, who were feeding her with fresh grass (which I thought she treated somewhat disdainfully), sugar-cane, and plantains. She was richly caparisoned in cloth of gold and ornaments, some of which she tore away, and was chastised for the offense by a blow on the proboscis by one of the keepers. She was fastened to an upright pole by ropes covered with scarlet cloth, but at night was released, had the liberty of the room, and slept against a matted and ornamental partition sloping from the floor at about an angle of forty-five degrees... The prince fed the elephant with sugar-cane, which appeared her favorite food; the grass she rather seemed disposed to toss about than to eat. The elephant had been trained to make a salaam by lifting her proboscis over the neck, and did so more than once at the prince's bidding."

Among the presents King Mongkut sent to Queen Victoria was a tuft of hair from the elephant, and Bowring was honored with a few hairs from the tail; portraits of the auspicious animal were presented to members of Bowring's suite as souvenirs of their stay.

Unfortunately, the elephant died later that year, plunging the court into mourning. As as a mark of royal favor, "from a beloved and faithful friend," the king sent Bowring a portion of its skin, "with beautiful body-hairs preserved in spirits." Bowring in turn, perhaps in the spirit of science, gave the skin to the museum of the Zoological Society of London. (Other portions are on display in the Royal Elephant Museum in Bangkok, along with a model of the raft used to transport such animals down the river.)

As historians have shown, the memoirs of Anna Leonowens, of "The King and I" fame, are not to be wholly trusted; but she was probably not straying too far from the truth when she wrote of the discovery of another white elephant in 1862:

"A temporary pavilion of extraordinary splendor sprang up, as if by magic, before the eastern gate of the palace; and the whole nation was wild with joy; when suddenly came awful tidings, - he had died!

"No man dared tell the king. But the Kralahome [Prime Minister] - that man of prompt expedients and unfailing presence of mind - commanded that the preparations should cease instantly, and that the building should vanish with the builders. In the evening his Majesty came forth, as usual, to exult in the glorious work. What was his astonishment to find no vestige of the splendid structure

Opposite: Model of raft used to transport white elephants during King Rama V's reign. (Royal Elephant National Museum)
Above: Preserved skin of a white elephant found in the reign of King Rama IV. (Royal Elephant National Museum)

that had been so nearly completed the night before. He turned, bewildered, to his courtiers, to demand an explanation, when suddenly the terrible truth flashed into his mind. With a cry of pain he sank down upon a stone, and gave vent to an hysterical passion of tears; but was presently consoled by one of his children, who, carefully prompted in his part, knelt before him and said: 'Weep not, O my father! The stranger lord may have left us but for a time.' The stranger lord, fatally pampered, had succumbed to astonishment and indigestion.

"A few days after this mournful event the king read to me a curious description of the defunct monster, and showed me parts of his skin preserved, and his tusks, which in size and whiteness surpassed the finest I have ever seen. 'His (that is, the elephant's) eyes were light blue, surrounded by salmon-color; his hair fine, soft, and white; his complexion pinkish white; his tusks like long pearls; his ears like silver shields; his trunk like a comet's tail; his legs like the feet of the skies; his tread like the sound of thunder; his looks full of meditation; his expression full of tenderness; his voice the voice of a mighty warrior; and his bearing that of an illustrious monarch.'"

(Anna may have acquired the information about the cause of the elephant's death

from the writings of the explorer and naturalist Henri Mouhot, which were published before she assembled her own memoirs. On a journey from Khorat to Bangkok in 1861, Mouhot wrote his brother, "I travelled in company with an animal who has a title equal to that of the greatest Siamese mandarin, and who was served by two inferior mandarins, who gave him his meals composed of cakes, biscuits, and sweetmeats out of golden dishes; and who had slaves sent before him to clear the way and cut down the brushwood and branches, for this elephant, according to the Siamese superstition and ignorance, possesses the soul of some deceased prince or king. They called him a white elephant, but in reality he had only a few spots of that color on his body. Alas! The king and all his mandarins are now in mourning, for the object of their worship died of indigestion. Poor beast and poor king!")

Most white elephants are born in the wild and their discovery is more or less accidental. In May of 1926, however, one appeared in a herd near Chiang Mai belonging to the Borneo Company, which had a teak concession there. It was a male, and at the age of four months, together with his mother, he was moved to a village closer to the city and formally examined

Above: Model of Phra Sawet Voralaksna, a white elephant belonging to King Rama V. (Royal Elephant National Museum)
Opposite: Shrine at White Elephant Gate in Chiang Mai.

Honors Paid to the White Elephant

Anna Leonowens became world-famous as the heroine of "The King and I," a popular musical comedy based very loosely on her memoirs The English Governess at the Siamese Court. *Historians have not been kind to her accuracy, especially her portrait of King Mongkut (Rama IV), but on such subjects as the white elephant - which she translates as* Chang Phoouk - *she seems to have drawn on reliable sources. The following excerpt uses her original spellings:*

"From the earliest times the kings of Siam and Birmah have anxiously sought for the white elephant, and having had the rare fortune to procure one, have loaded it with gifts and dignities, as though it were a conscious favorite of the throne. When the governor of a province in Siam is notified of the appearance of a white elephant within his baliwick, he immediately commands that prayers and offerings shall be made in all the temples, while he sends out a formidable expedition of hunters and slaves to take the precious beast, and bring it in triumph. As soon as he is informed of its capture, a special messenger is dispatched to inform the king of its sex, probable age, size, complexion, deportment, looks, and ways; and in the presence of his Majesty this bearer of glorious tidings undergoes the painfully pleasant operation of having his mouth, ears, and nostrils stuffed with gold. Especially is the lucky wight— perhaps some half-wild woodsman— who was first to spy the illustrious monster munificently rewarded. Orders are promptly issued to the *woons* and the *wongses* [i.e., officials] of the several districts through which he must pass to prepare to receive him royally, and a wide path is cut for him through the forests he must traverse on his way to the capital. Wherever he rests he is sumptuously entertained, and everywhere he is escorted and served by a host of attendants, who sing, dance, play upon instruments, and perform feats of strength or skill for his amusement, until he reaches the banks of the Meinam, where a great floating palace of wood, surmounted by a gorgeous roof and hung with crimson curtains, awaits him. The roof is literally thatched with flowers ingeniously arranged so as to form symbols and mottoes, which the superior beast is supposed to decipher with ease. The floor of this splendid float is laid with gilt matting curiously woven, in the center of which his four-footed lordship is installed in state, surrounded by an obsequious and enraptured crowd of mere bipeds, who bathe him, perfume him, fan him, feed him, sing and play to him, flatter him. His food consists of the finest herbs, the tenderest grass, the sweetest sugar-cane, the mellowest plantains, the brownest cakes of wheat, served on huge trays of gold and silver; and his drink is perfumed with the fragrant flower of the *aok malee*, the large native jessamine.

"Thus, in more than princely state, he is floated down the river to a point within seventy miles of the capital, where the king and his court, all the chief personages of the kingdom, and a multitude of priests, both Buddhist and Brahmin, accompanied by troops of players and musicians, come out to meet him and conduct him with honors to his stable-palace. A great number of cords and ropes of all qualities and lengths are attached to the raft, those in the center being of fine silk (figuratively, 'spun from a spider's web'). These are for the king and his noble retinue, who with their own hands make them fast to their gilded barges; the rest are secured to the great fleet of lesser boats. And so, with shouts of joy, beating of drums, blare of trumpets, boom of cannon, a hallelujah of music, and various splendid revelry, the great *Chang Phoouk* is conducted in triumph to the capital."

by the Prince of Chiang Mai, who pronounced conformity with all the rules governing such auspicious creatures.

On October 14, the baby elephant formally entered Chiang Mai via the Pratu Chang Pheuak, the White Elephant Gate, a portal steeped in local legend. Through the same entrance, in the 14th century, another white elephant passed bearing sacred relics of the Buddha placed in a howdah on its back. It proceeded to climb Doi Suthep, the low mountain overlooking Chiang Mai, stopping only when it reached a spot near the summit, where it trumpeted, turned around three times, and reverently knelt; a *chedi* was built there to enshrine the relics and later the famous Wat Phra That, still a major destination for Buddhist pilgrims.

The young elephant found in 1926 passed through the the city in a splendid procession, led by two of the Prince's most beautiful elephants and followed by thirteen others, finally leaving through another set of gates, Pratu Tha Pae. "Tired from such a long journey," wrote Raymond Plion-Bernier, a Frenchman who witnessed the celebration, "deafened by the noise, the unhappy animal undoubtedly thought his torment was at an end when he reached the gardens of the Borneo Company which had been prepared to receive him. The sun descending behind the mountain, the shade of the palm trees and the freshness of the nearby river incited thoughts of rest. But greatness brings with it obligations... His worries had only just begun. First of all he was given a shower of lustral water which, after all, must not have seemed so disagreeable, after so much dust and heat. Then he was religiously covered with cooked rice and flower petals which made him for a short moment, truly white. But shaken off in anger and in contempt of the most sacred rites, this white covering quickly disappeared. Eager to contribute to the annoyances which were overwhelming the baby elephant, the Chao Luang [Prince] approached him slyly and, before he could put up the slightest resistance, draped around his neck a necklace of flowers which appeared to bother him considerably. The rites of Riek Khwan require that an appeal be made in this manner to the good-naturedness of the guardian spirit of the elephant. At long last he and his mother - who had had her own share of honors and annoyances - were permitted to enjoy some sugar canes and banana leaves presented to them in a silver bowl."

The next day the white elephant made another ceremonial trip through the town, this time ultimately finding refuge at an estate belonging to the Chao Luang at the foot of Doi Suthep. There he was allowed to rest three months before an even greater event.

After many years of work, the northern railway line had finally reached Chiang Mai, dramatically opening the once-remote city to easy access from Bangkok. Their Majesties King Prajadhipok and Queen Rambhai Barni were scheduled to travel on the new line, and D.F. Macfie, the Manager of the Borneo Company, had arranged a private ceremony to present the new white elephant to them during their historic visit, the first by a Thai king to the province.

Opposite: Entry of King Rama VII into Chiang Mai, 1926. (Courtesy of National Archives)
Following spread: Procession of white elephants. (Courtesy of National Archives)

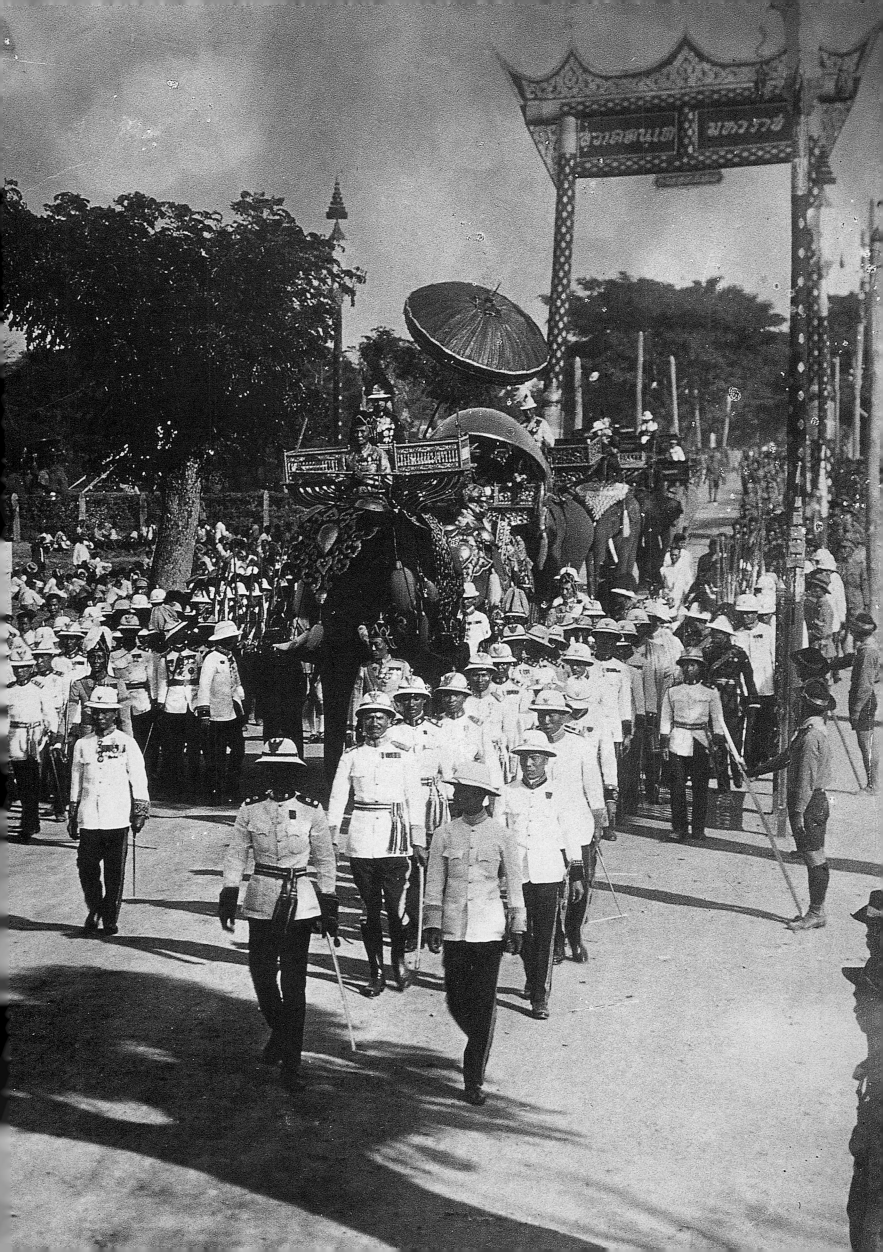

It was perhaps the last grand elephant display in Chiang Mai. "On that occasion," W.A.R. Wood remembered, "Their Majesties entered the city with a procession which included eighty-four

elephants, among them four Consular elephants belonging to King George V of England. A great deal of time was spent in training the elephants for this procession, as it included several bands of various kinds, and many elephants tend to bolt when they hear unaccustomed noises. For a fortnight ahead the eighty-four elephants had to have drums beaten and trumpets blown close to their ears and those which showed an obstinate dislike of these sounds were relegated to the tail end of the procession. We were all rather nervous when the King arrived, fearing that, even after their intensive musical training, some of the elephants might bolt and throw the whole cortege into confusion; but it all went off very well, and if the procession pleased the King and Queen as much as it did the loyal citizens of Chiang Mai, they must have been feeling very happy."

The object of all the attention also provoked some worry. "It was in a very frisky mood," Wood recalled, "and during the course of the preliminary proceedings knocked Mr. Macfie down and pushed me and two other men into a ditch. We were all very nervous about its first meeting with the King and Queen, as it would never have done for the young elephant to behave roughly towards them, and men were standing all around prepared forcibly to quell the rampageous infant if it showed the slightest signs of being naughty. As it turned out, the behavior of the little elephant was perfect; one might almost have supposed that it knew it was in the presence of royalty. The King offered it a piece of sugar cane, whereupon it raised its little trunk, as though in salutation, and then accepted the dainty in the quietest and politest fashion."

But the elephant's social tribulations were not over yet. In November of that year it became the first white elephant to travel by railway, in a special coach equipped with electric fans and lights, showers, and even a telephone, built for him and his mother. H.R.H. Prince Purachatra, the Minister of Commerce and Communications, came to oversee preparations for the journey, which took a full week instead of the usual twenty-four hours due to frequent stops along the way so that admirers could present offerings. The two elephants finally reached Chitralada Station at 4 PM on November 15th, were greeted by the King and other dignitaries, and ultimately, after several more days of ceremonies and festivities, installed in a special pavilion on the palace grounds.

"For three days," wrote M. Plion-Bernier, "the public was allowed to present their respects to the sacred animal and to offer sugar canes, bananas, and other appropriate nourishment to him and his mother. To see one's offering accepted was considered a sign of celestial goodwill and the messenger from heaven certainly did not reveal himself chary of his favors, at the risk of indigestion, as had been the case one or two times in the past."

(Macfie, who presented the animal to the king, was rewarded with the Order of the White Elephant; he subsequently retired in Chiang Mai, was interned as an enemy alien during World War Two, and died in 1945.)

The overthrow of the absolute monarchy in 1932, as well as the political turmoil and war that followed, appeared for a time to dim the luster of the white elephant cult. Even before then, it had ceased to appear prominently as a symbol of the kingdom against a red background on the national flag, originally devised by King Rama II. According to one explanation, the change came as the result of a trip King Vajiravudh (Rama VI) made to Uthai Thani Province in 1916. Since elephant flags were expensive, many households thriftily flew red and white streamers instead; more disturbingly, one house which did have a proper flag was flying it upside down. The King, it is said, thereupon determined to adopt a new flag and devised the present one in 1917. (Others have suggested that he did so because he regarded the old flag as too exotic for a progressive kingdom like the one he was striving to create. 'To most people," he is reported as having once commented, "Siam is a country full of White Elephants and nothing much besides." It might also be worth noting that one of the white elephants found during his reign was anything but the gentle and dignified creature of legend; it went on several rampages in Bangkok, smashing rickshaws and even automobiles. and finally drowned when it became jammed between a pontoon and the river bank.)

Opposite: King Rama VII entering Chiang Mai. (Courtesy of National Archives)
Above: A royal white elephant. (Courtesy of National Archives)

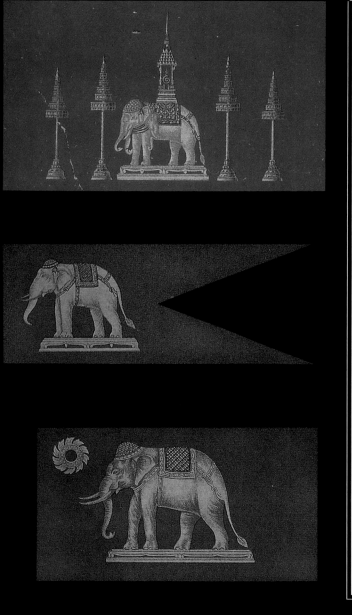

Origin of the Flag of Siam

In ancient times, plain colored flags were used when Siamese armies went into battle to distinguish them from opposing forces. This was also the case for trading boats when they went to other kingdoms; during the Ayutthaya period, for example a plain red flag was used by Siamese merchant boats.

Early in the Rattanakosin (Bangkok) era, a trading post was established by the British in Singapore, and two royal ships built by King Rama II, displaying the red flag, went there and to Macao to trade. Eventually the English governer-general of Singapore sent an officer informing the King that commercial boats from Malaya displayed a similar flag and asking him if another could be used so that royal ships could be distinguished and received in a proper manner.

As it happened, King Rama II had just received three white elephants and thus he ordered that an image of the auspicious animal be put on the flag, symbolizing the King Who Owned White Elephants.

During the reign of King Rama IV the royal decoration known as the Order of the White Elephant was created to honor those who gave outstanding service to the kingdom.

Opposite page from top: The King's colors; the Commodore's pennant; the Admiral's flag; former flag of Siam.

This page: Royal Decorations.
Top: Knight Grand Cross of the Most Exalted Order of the White Elephant. *Left:* Knight Grand Cordon (Special Class).
Above: Engraving of the Collar, Badge and Star of the Royal Order of the White Elephant.

Traditionally royal white elephants had been kept within the compound of the Grand Palace, in stables located on the site of the present Maha Chakri Prasat, and taken for their regular baths in the nearby river. Toward the end of the nineteenth century, King Chulalongkorn (Rama V) began construction of a new palace in the Dusit district, which was to be surrounded by a new city of parks and broad avenues modelled after those he had seen in Europe. Some stables were built during this reign for the elephants near the Dusit Throne Hall, and these were later expanded by King Rama VII. After the change of government in 1932, the royal elephants were moved to a special pavilion at Khao Din Zoo, across the street from the Dusit stables, where they were displayed until the 1960s when they were moved again, this time to the more private grounds of Chitralada Palace; the stables were opened as an elephant museum in the 1980s.

That the belief was by no means a quaint relic of the past, though, has been shown in the present reign, during which an unprecedented total of ten of the highest rank and six of lesser quality but still auspicious have been identified and added to the royal collection, which seems only appropriate for the longest-reigning monarch in the world today.

The first white elephant to be found after King Bhumibol Adulyadej came to the throne was placed in the zoo, while a second, in Chiang Mai, died young. The third was discovered in Yala Province in the 1960s. It was alone in the jungle, a very unusual occurence since baby elephants are normally well taken care of by their mothers and other females of the herd. It readily followed the village *kamnan's* elephant back to a village, where for the next twenty days it stayed in the *kamnan's* compound and revealed a number of unusual traits. It was very affectionate to people, especially children, and moreover the *kamnan's* own elephant seemed to be afraid of it and stayed as far away as possible. Feelings grew that it might be a white elephant, whereupon it was moved to the grounds of the provincial governor's residence and eventually the Royal Household Bureau was notified of the discovery.

An eighty-year-old expert, who had been with the court since the reign of King Chulalongkorn and who had examined more than fifty alleged white elephants, was dispatched to Yala. The examination took a month, at the end of which the young male was declared to belong to the first subdivision of the first class - in other words, the very highest.

The elephant was given the name Phra Savet Adulyadej Pahon, which was engraved on a piece of red sugar cane given to

Above: Phra Savet Adulyadej Pahon, one of the royal white elephants of the highest rank at Chitralada Palace

him when Their Majesties the King and Queen came to the southern province in May 1968 for the ceremonies of investiture. The full name, however, was quite long, partially translated by one writer as "an offering of the gods. Having pink eyes and being of the first order it is sent for service to the King and the good fortune of the Thai people."

The ceremonies, presided over by a Brahmin priest assisted by six other Brahmins, lasted four and a half days. On the first day it rained, ending a two-month drought, a clearly auspicious sign. On the second there was a gala parade during which the baby elephant wore a headdress and a gold brocaded coverlet bestowed by the King, accompanied by a retinue in traditional costumes. This was followed by a day-long cultural show and then, at last, religious rites during which the King poured lustral water over the elephant and gave him the sugar cane bearing his name, thus ensuring that he would never forget it.

Today, regarded as one of the two finest white elephants found un-

der the Chakri Dynasty - the other was during the reign of King Chulalongkorn - Phra Savet Adulyadej Pahon lives in a pavilion of his own, treated with respect but also with some caution as he is known to be far less docile than the other royal elephants.

A new project, initiated in 1986, calls for the gradual move of the white and 'important' elephants out of their relatively confined quarters at Chitralada Palace to more open territory near palaces maintained by Their Majesties in provincial areas, thus improving their health while conforming to the tradition that such animals must live in royal surroundings. The first, an 'important' specimen named Palai Yod Phetch, went to the Elephant Training Center at Lampang the following year, and two more were sent in 1988.

M.L. Phiphatanachatr Diskul, a veterinarian who works with the Royal Chitralada Projects, was quoted in an interview as saying "When they were released into their new habitat, [they] acted like children seeing a new world for the first time. At first

Above: Royal white elephants at Chitralada Palace being exercised.

they didn't want to stray far from the people who cared for them. Wherever their keepers went, the elephants followed. If the keeper went into a lavatory, the elephant waited patiently outside. If an elephant was eating grass and looked up to find its keeper missing, it would lift up its head and bray with fear... But gradually they began to adjust. They learned to pick leaves for themselves, to climb inclines securely, and they became visibly happier and more confident. One important thing we observed was that their muscle tone became very good. White elephants are beautiful animals, but in the city it was often hard to appreciate this because they got so little exercise and they weren't in good condition. But after they had lived in a natural environment for a while, exercise restored them to their proper proportions. When you saw them, you realized why white elephants are considered special, and how they differ from ordinary ones."

Information on the relocated elephants was presented to His Majesty the King in 1992. As a result, new residences were established in Sakon Nakhon Province and two white elephants transferred there in 1994; another two followed them in 1996. The elephants sent to Lampang were moved to a residence constructed at the Elephant Conservation Center in that province, where they were joined by two more.

The ultimate goal, according to M.L. Phiphatanachatr, was to move all the Chitralada white elephants to more salubrious surroundings. "But we must always keep the old Thai traditions in mind," he said. "If an elephant is to be moved, we must conduct the appropriate Brahmin ceremony to tell the animal's protecting god. When it enters its new habitat, a ceremony must be held to request the permission of the gates of the forest to admit the elephant. And when the elephant is being transported, it must be done in the proper way."

Thus it appears that Thailand's white elephant will continue to be a living symbol rather than an exotic subject for artists and imaginative writers.

Opposite: A royal white elephant.
Above: White elephants bathing at Chitralada Palace.

The Royal Elephant National Museum

Bangkok has numerous specialized museums that appear in few guidebooks and are seldom seen by the average tourist. There is one, for instance, devoted to crime (displaying the preserved bodies of several famous murderers), as well as one with exhibits of old methods of punishment. Yet another that deserves greater popularity among visitors is the Royal Elephant National Museum, where the primary focus is on illustrious white elephants found during the present Chakri Dynasty but that also offers many other fascinating items associated with elephants in general.

Under the first four Chakri kings, white elephants were kept in stables at the Grand Palace and took part in many of the ceremonies held within that dazzling center of secular and spiritual power. By the fifth reign, however, the palace was becoming overcrowded, and King Chulalongkorn perceived the need for a new royal residence with room for expansion. He selected the Dusit District, north of the palace, where he began construction of a new series of buildings that would include the magnificent Anantasamakhum

Throne Hall, together with a number of royal palaces and parks, plazas, and broad avenues laid out in European style.

As part of this plan, stables were built for the royal elephants (later expanded during the reign of King Rama VII) in an area to the left of the throne hall and behind the golden-teak Vimarn Mek palace. Here the auspicious elephants were kept until after the end of the absolute monarchy in 1932, when they were moved first to special pavilions in Khao Din Zoo and later to the grounds of Chitralada Palace, residence of the present King. There was some talk of destroying the elephant stables when plans were drawn up for a new Parliament building nearby, but this was fortunately stilled when the Fine Arts Department declared them an important cultural site in 1974; the buildings were restored with private donations and formally opened as the Royal Elephant National Museum on the occasion of Her Majesty the Queen's sixtieth birthday in 1992.

The two Thai-style buildings that comprise the museum look out on the beautifully landscaped gardens of

Vimarn Mek, not far from the Victorian structure that displays items made by Her Majesty's SUPPORT Foundation; on the other side, across the street, visitors can glimpse that part of Khao Din Zoo where a number of ordinary elephants still browse in several elegant pavilions originally built for auspicious members of their tribe.

Dominating the first building are a number of enormous tusks from white elephants that belonged to early Chakri kings— it was the custom to mount and display such relics after the death of the animals— along with small models of particular favorites, mostly found in the fourth and fifth reigns, as well as paintings of auspicious elephants, old photographs of ceremonies and elephant roundups, and statues of the elephant god Ganesha (among them a stone image brought back from Java by King Chulalongkorn). Reproductions from classic manuscript books show such legendary elephant categories as Brahmapong, Sivapong, Vishnupong, and Agnipong, with explanations of the benefits they bring to their possessors. Display cabinets around the room are filled with a fascinating collection of traditional items associated with elephants and their care.

In one, for instance, are sections of preserved skin from a beloved white elephant that died in the reign of King Mongkut (Rama IV), perhaps the same

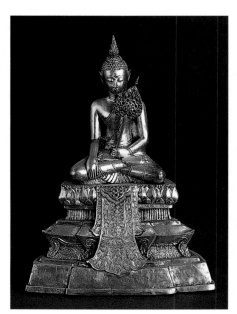

one from which the King sent Sir John Bowring a similar piece, remarking that the gift came "from a beloved and faithful friend." Nearby are ivory-handled brushes made from the hair or tails of auspicious elephants, yantras (magic formulas) used in the installation ceremony for such animals, and a necklace-amulet fashioned of palm leaves to put around a white elephant's neck.

Still other cabinets display accessories used in rounding up wild elephants, amulets favored by mahouts, an immense elephant molar tooth, and a model of a spacious barge used to bring a newly-discovered white elephant down the Chao Phraya River during King Chulalongkorn's reign.

In the second pavilion stands the realistic, life-sized image of a white elephant found in the present reign, adorned with the rich trappings it wore on ceremonial occasions. Also on view are models of a white monkey and a white crow, also regarded as auspicious animals, and traditional musical instruments played during the rituals to consecrate an illustrious elephant.

For anyone interested in Thailand's ancient culture in general, and elephants in particular, the Royal Elephant National Museum is a trove of unusual information and relics.

Opposite page : The Royal Elephant National Museum.

This page, top: Victory Buddha; when going to war the kings of Siam would install this image on an elephant's back to accompany the army into battle. *Above:* Ceremonial dagger with ivory handle of Ganesha, belonging to the Kui people. *Right:* Tassel of hair from royal elephants made into brushes and whisks with ivory handles.

Opposite: Pair of wooden white elephant votive figures; height 29.5 cm. (Collection of Pratin Hetrakul)
Above: Double-sided carving of a white elephant. (Private Collection)
Following spread: Antique crouching elephant, wood; height 31 cm. (Collection of Pratin Hetrakul)

Above: Stucco work at Wat Lai, Lopburi, a fine example of early Ayutthaya craftsmanship (17th century).
The scene depicts the seige of the city of Mitira, an episode from one of the Buddhist Jatakas.

Elephants in Art and Legend

The immense size and distinctive shape of the elephant, combined with deep-rooted beliefs regarding its power, longevity, and sagacity, have guaranteed it a prominent place both in legend and in works of art throughout the history of mankind. It appears as a subject in many prehistoric cave paintings, on ancient coins and medals, in statuary, as a textile motif, sometimes in places far from what we regard today as the animal's natural habitat. A large Islamic silk hanging known as the "Shroud of St. Jossee," dating from the mid-tenth century and brought to France after the first Crusade, shows a row of chunky elephants in red, yellow, and brown, along with a border of camels, while a fifteenth-century manuscript in the British Museum offers a fanciful pair with turned-up tusks, straight trunks that resemble telescopes, and hooves instead of feet.

It is not surprising, then, to find that these artistic expressions are particularly strong in Thailand, where the elephant has always been a part of the landscape. Terra cotta figures of the animal have been found among the relics of Ban Chiang, a prehistoric culture that flourished on the northeastern plateau, and it was an important figure in nearly all the varied influences that have shaped Thai culture over the centuries.

Hindu legends, for example, brought by early Indian traders and also absorbed through Khmer influence, abound in stories concerning the animal. According to one, eight male and eight female elephants emerged from a 'cosmic egg' when commanded to do so by the Creator; at first, it is said, they possessed the power of flight but lost it due to the curse of a hermit when they landed in a banyan tree and accidentally crushed his hut. Another claims that a magical lotus emerged from the abdomen of the god Vishnu (Narai or Narayana in the Thai version) while he was sleeping on the cosmic sea; using the pollen from this blossom, Vishnu, Siva, Agni, and Brahma created

Opposite: Gold and red mural at Wat Prasat in Chiang Mai showing an event in the Buddha's life.
Above: Incised brick from Chiang Saen period depicting an episode from the Vessantara Jataka. (Chiang Saen National Museum)

ninety groups of celestial elephants, the ancestors of those on earth today.

Many stories, including the epic Ramayana (Ramakien in Thailand) also concern Erawan (from the Sanskrit *airavana* or *airavata*), a white elephant divinity and mount of the god Indra; he generally appears with three heads, though sometimes he may have thirty-three, representing the various heavenly states. Another popular legendary character is Ganesha, the part-elephant son of Siva and Pavarti, regarded as the Remover of Obstacles and the Lord of Beginnings, especially revered by artisans and those involved in capturing, training, and keeping elephants.

Strange creatures from Hindu mythology, in which elephantine features were combined with those of birds, lions, and fish, also found their way into Thai culture, sometimes losing their original names and roles in the process but retaining their odd appearances.

Buddhism, as we have seen in previous chapters, adopted the animal as a prominent symbol. This was particularly true in Sri Lanka, where Theravada Buddhism spread from India in the 3rd century B.C. and from which the faith came to Thailand. According to myth, the Buddhist scriptures were first sent to Sri Lanka from India on a ship, tied to the

back of an elephant; when the vessel capsized in a storm, the brave animal swam the rest of the way and saved its precious cargo, thus earning a special place in local lore and affection.

Elephants figure in many episodes of the Buddha's life story. An auspicious white elephant appears to the Buddha's royal mother just before she gives birth; in his epic struggle to attain enlightenment, the wicked god Mara rides a fearsome war elephant; and in yet another familiar story, when he tires of quarrelling monks and seeks refuge in the forest, an elephant and a monkey come to offer solace to him.

Elephants appear, too, in the moralistic Jataka tales recounting the Buddha's previous existences. The most popular of these stories in Thailand, depicted in countless temple murals, manuscripts, and paintings on cloth, is the story of Prince Vessantara, who demonstrates his charitable nature by giving away all his possessions, including a beloved white elephant; at the end, his virtue triumphant, Vessantara and his wife return to their palace escorted by a splendid procession of elephants.

During the Sukhothai period, Thai missionary monks went to Sri Lanka, by then the foremost center of Buddhist scholarship. One monk, Sisatta, is said to have resided there for a

Opposite and above: Two depictions of the same scene from the life of the Buddha; having gone to the forest to escape the distraction of quarelling monks, the Buddha is offered sustenance by an elephant and a white monkey. (Collection of Victor Sassoon and Chiang Saen National Museum)

long time, to have helped in the building of Sri Lanka's holiest stupa at Anuradhapura, and, when he returned to Thailand, to have brought not only relics of the Buddha but also artisans who introduced new techniques and motifs. One of the latter was an elephant buttress appearing at the base of monuments This may have originated in an Indian myth which held that the dome-shaped universe rested on the broad backs of celestial elephants and which had been adapted by Sri Lankan Buddhist architects who had their own reasons for admiring the animal. In any case, the design influenced a number of important structures in Thailand. The most famous of these is Wat Chang Lom ("the temple circled with elephants") in Si Satchanalai, where thirty-six life-sized elephants made of stuccoed laterite surround the central stupa; the same motif can be found in other places, among them Wat Chang Rob in Kamphaeng Phet, where the figures are adorned with jewelry, and also on some Ayutthaya monuments.

(In more recent years, it might be noted, Thailand's spiritual debt to Sri Lanka has been repaid in part by the donation of several elephants who take part in the famous festival held every year at Kandy to celebrate a Sacred Tooth of the Buddha.)

As shown by the Ramkhamhaeng inscription already mentioned, the elephant was an integral part of Sukhothai's daily life, and thus it is not surprising to find it commonly rendered in local kilns as votive figures and oil lamps, often in a sea-green celadon glaze, as well as in stucco decorations.

Even the famous three-dimensional Walking Buddha of Thailand's first capital, called by Alexander Griswold "the most astonishing invention of Sukhothai sculpture and the glory of Thai art," derived at least one of its features from the elephant, as artisans sought to follow an esoteric Pali canon taught in Sri Lanka. The ideal was summarized by Griswold as follows: "The legs are like the legs of a deer, and the thighs like the stems of banana trees. The arms are smooth and rounded, like the trunk of an elephant;

Above: Bejeweled elephant figures at Wat Chang Rob in Kamphaeng Phet. *Opposite:* Figure of an elephant with riders and soldiers guarding each leg; Sangkalok stoneware with celadon glaze, mid-14th to early 16th centuries, height 24.5 cm. (Collection of Professor Arun Chaiseri)

Opposite: Wat Sorasak in Sukhothai, now restored, the elephants are made of laterite covered with stucco.
This page from top left: Wat Hua Nong in Wiang Kum Kam, an ancient moated town founded by King Mengrai;
ruins of the stupa of Wat Chedi Luang built in 1401 in Chiang Mai; Wat Chang Lom in Si Satchanalai; base of the stupa of
Wat Chedi Si Hong in Sukhothai; Wat Mahevong in Ayutthaya, built during the reign of King Borommaracha II (142ʿ-48).

Opposite: Figure of elephant with mahout and musicians; Sangkalok stoneware, mid-14th to early 16th centuries; height 25 cm.
This page from top: Pair of candle holders from Sukhothai period; glazed, height 10 cm.; Water vessel with painted under-glaze, height 14 cm.; Khmer vessel with lid; glazed with incised decoration, height 23 cm. (All collection of Prof. Arun Chaiser)

the hands are like lotus flowers just before beginning to open, with the fingertips turning backward like petals. The shape of the head is like an egg; the chin, with its incised oval line, is like a mango stone; the nose is like a parrot's beak, and the eyebrows like drawn bows." (This association of the trunk with sinuous grace was also carried over into literature; in a poem called "The Legend of the Rose," King Rama VI of the present Chakri Dynasty describes the heroine's arms as moving "smoothly like the dancing trunk of an elephant.")

The *Traibumikatha (The Story of the Three Planes of Existence)*, generally regarded as the first example of Thai Buddhist literature, was produced in the reign of King Lithai, Sukhothai's fifth ruler. Elephants described in this great work include certain auspicious specimens, possession of which is a mark of the Universal King: "They are white of color, like the glow of the moon in its full glory. The soles of their feet are rosy like the sun at first dawning. Their feet bear the nine marks of beauty, and are as perfect as if sculpted by artists. Their trunks are as red as the red lotus bloom. They move swiftly through the sky like an Airavana (Erawan) possessed of supernatural powers."

It is said by one writer, F.H. Giles, in an article written for the *Siam Society Journal*, that ancient Thai elephants inspired music: "After the capture of a white or noble and distinguished animal, lullabies were composed and sung to make it sleep, the theme of the composition being in praise of its high qualities, and eulogies were also sung to wean it from the craving for the forest life. This curious practice has the sanction of antiquity, for Megasthenes, a Greek ambassador at the court of the Hindu Emperor Chandragupta, about 300 B.C., whose capital was at Pataliputra (modern Patna), records that the Indians sang songs to the accompaniment of music to soothe and coax wild elephants recently captured."

Indian mythology is reflected in many of the Khmer monuments of Thailand's northeastern region, once part of the Angkorian empire. The rounded towers, or *prangs*, represent the sacred Mount Meru - center of both the Hindu and Buddhist universes - and are decorated with numerous stone carvings that show elephants alone, in royal processions, or in some celestial form like the Erawan. Such motifs were assimilated into Thai art and can be found on such temples as Wat Arun on the Chao Phraya River in Bangkok, where Indra mounted on Erawan faces the four cardinal points on the central *prang*.

Opposite: Detail of stone lintel at Prasat Hin Phanom Rung, one of the most important Khmer monuments in Thailand.
Above: Indra is known as the god who protects the eastern side and is often found on pediments and lintels facing that direction, as shown here at Prasat Ban Phluang, an 11th century Baphuon-style Khmer sanctuary near Surin.

Items surviving from the 400-year rule of Ayutthaya attest not only to the refined skills that characterized that splendid kingdom but also to the continuing appeal of the elephant. One of the most famous examples was part of a collection of royal possessions discovered at Wat Rajburana, built in 1424 by King Baromaracha II to honor two of his brothers who had been killed in a duel on elephant back; hidden in a secret crypt within the temple's Khmer-style *prang*, the objects remained undiscovered until the 1950s, nearly two centuries after the city's destruction. The find included more than 600 Buddha images, over 100,000 votive tablets, and an extraordinary trove of items crafted in gold. Among the latter was an exquisite little crouching elephant adorned with gemstones, bearing an ornate howdah on its back and reverently holding up a bejewelled offering in its trunk.

Other art that flourished in Ayutthaya were gold-and-black lacquer painting, mother-of-pearl inlay, woodcarving, temple murals, and illustrated manuscript books. The most common subjects for painting were events in the Life of the Buddha, the Jataka tales (particularly the last ten), and the Three Planes of Existence, in all of which elephants appear either as heavenly creatures or taking part in any number of earthly tasks. Illustrated manuscript books also treated less exalted subjects such as the use of elephants in warfare and methods of training them.

In Lanna Thai, a separate kingdom that evolved in the north between the thirteenth and fourteenth centuries, elephants served as vital transport in the largely roadless mountains and also figured in local legends. It was a sacred white elephant that bore relics of the Buddha up Doi Suthep and marked the location of a celebrated temple, where a statue of him now stands as a reminder of the great event, and the Chiang Mai gate through which he passed has ever since been known as Pratu Chang Pheuak.

Skilled woodcarvers of the region regularly depicted elephants in their decorations for temples, while ordinary people adorned bullock carts with a back panel on which the animal is shown in profile. In the north, the elephant replaces the

This page top: Some of the gold objects found at Wat Rajburana in Ayutthaya, (Chao Sam Phraya National Museum, Ayutthaya)
This page bottom: Stone sculpture of elephant uncovered in Phayao, a sovereign kingdom which was annexed in 1338 to the Lanna kingdom. (Chiang Saen National Museum)
Opposite: 'Sattaphan' candle holder in Haripunchai (Lamphun) style. (Collection of Mae Fah Luang Foundation)
Following spread: Wooden carving from the facade of a Lanna temple. (Collection of The Siam Society)

The Elephant in Thai Literature

Elephants figure prominently in a number of Thai literary works, among them the following.

Samutakot Kam Chan

This great work of literature was written by three poets. It was begun during the reign of King Narai (1656-1688) by Phra Maha Ratcha Khru, the chief Brahmin priest who officiated at state rituals, who died when the work was half done. The King then wrote additional verses but the poem was completed by the Supreme Patriarch Prince Poramanuchit Chinorot in 1849, during the reign of King Rama III.

Based on the Sanutakot Jataka, one of the moralistic tales of the Buddha's previous existences, the poem reflects King Narai's keen interest in elephants. The favorite sport of the hero, Phra Samutakot, is capturing elephants, and there is also a scene in which a senior mahout performs the necessary rituals before going into the forest on such a trip. In addition, there are descriptions of thirty-four types of inauspicious elephants, the eight families of auspicious elephants created by Brahma, and the ten families of earthly elephants.

Unarut

This is a verse play written by King Rama I, who established Bangkok as the capital and led a revival of classical Thai arts. One scene decribes the hero, Prince Unarut, enjoying himself by roping wild elephants, a royal sport that went far back in the kingdom's history.

Lilit Taleng Phat (Victory Over the Burmese)

Written by the Supreme Patriarch Prince Paramanuchit Chinorot in the reign of King Rama III, this is a poem that celebrates the victory of King Naresuan the Great over the Crown Prince of Burma at Don Chedi in 1592. The two fought on elephant back and in his description of the battle the poet compares King Naresuan's mount to Smithi Marong, an all-powerful elephant that resembles Indra's Erawan. The Crown Prince's elephant, by contrast, is compared to Kiri Mek, the mount of the evil Phya Vasavati who tempted the Buddha when he was seeking enlightenment.

The Ramakian

This was based on the Ramayana, the epic Sanskrit drama. Three versions have been written in the Ratanakosin Period, the first by poets and court scholars during the reign of King Rama I, the second by King Rama II, and the third by King Rama VI. In the second version, Erawan, mount of the god Indra, is fully described when one of the characters disguises himself as Indra and succeeds in fooling the white monkey Hanuman.

(Adapted from an article by Professor Suthilak Ambhanwong)

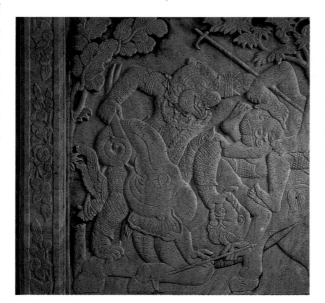

Opposite: Disguised as the god Indra, Indrachit leads an army through the sky n this Ramakien painting from King Rama V's reign. (Collection of Asst. Prof. Sone Simatrang) *Left:* Low-relief carving at Wat Po, Bangkok, depicting Hanuman, the monkey king, riding Erawan in another scene from the Ramakien.

pig among the twelve animals of the lunar cycle and can be found in many carvings and paintings devoted to these significant creatures. Wat Chang Kham Vora Viharn in Nan province, dating from 1406, has an elephant buttress similar to those of Sukhothai, as does Wat Chiang Man in Chiang Mai, believed to be the first temple built by the founder of the Lanna kingdom.

Northern Thailand, it should be noted, was a vassal state of Burma for two centuries, and the art and architecture of the region shows strong Burmese influence. Similarly, it is difficult to separate purely Thai elements from those of neighboring Laos and Cambodia in the northeast, where design motifs crossed borders as easily as the people did in the not so distant past.

If live elephants were never quite as ubiquitous in Bangkok as they had been in earlier capitals, they were no less omnipresent in its arts. One of the several objectives of King Rama I when he began construction of his new city in 1782 was to reflect the splendors of Ayutthaya, which then lay in still-fresh ruins, and all the skills and legends of the lost capital were employed in this. Part of Bangkok's lengthy official name is "city of angels, precious abode of Indra," which ensured plentiful depictions of the god (by

now a symbol of Thai royalty) and his fabulous elephant mount.

Within the precincts of the Grand Palace and its adjacent Temple of the Emerald Buddha, originally modeled after Ayutthaya buildings, elephants or reminders of them appear at almost every turn. There are royal insignia, such as that of King Rama II showing three white elephants; impressive tusks, sometimes elaborately carved, from former royal elephants; elegant pavilions which early kings used as places to change their regalia and as platforms from which to mount their elephants; and innumerable murals, carvings, and lacquer paintings in which the animal is featured.

The Chakri Maha Prasat, built during the fifth reign and reflecting the changing tastes of its time, is largely Western in architecture and decoration; but four elephant statues stand at the foot of its main stairway, a trio of them figure in the emblem of King Chulalongkorn above the entrance, and tusks and howdahs are displayed in the reception rooms. (The royal elephant stables were formerly located on the site of the Chakri Maha Prasat, and the name Tha Chang, a landing on the nearby river, is a reminder of the fact that the animals were once taken there for their regular bath.)

Above: Tung, or banner, hung outside temples on festival days, depicting animals of the lunar cycle. (Collection of Paothong Thongchua)
Opposite: Gold stenciled decorations on a pillar inside Wat Phumin, Nan province.

Opposite page: Wooden bracket and *chofa* (a horn-like finial at the roof-ends of monasteries) in the shape of a *hatsadiling*, or "bird carrying the mark of an elephant." (Collection of The Siam Society) *Small photo: Chofa* from a building near Chiang Mai.
This page, top row: Air vents from temples in the north; *Bottom row:* Wrought-iron grillwork; such grillwork, used on balconies and windows, was originally made in England but may have also been produced in Burma later. (Courtesy of Richard Dixon); Wooden bracket (Collection of The Siam Society); Decorative feature on a bargeboard from a northern temple. (Collection of Robert McCarthy)

Opposite top & middle: Elephant composites: sugarcane-cutter handle and Burmese ink container both in the shape of a *hatsadiling.*
Opposite bottom: Mural showing half-elephant half-fish from Wat Kongkaram, Rajburi.
This page: The *kotchasingh* - a mythical half-lion half-elephant depicted in Sangkalok pottery
and on stucco decorations at Wat Phra Singh, Chiang Mai.

173

This page & opposite: Art from the reign of King Rama III; rarely seen murals of a scripture repository at Wat Po in Bangkok serve as a treatise on elephants, horses, cats and astronomy. The top detail illustration shows maidens drawn in such a way they form the shape of an elephant.

Statues of white elephants belonging to Chakri monarchs are displayed in groups in the compound of the Emerald Buddha Temple, while on the gable of the Ho Phra Monthien (the Supplementary Library) Indra is shown astride Erawan, and war elephants move through the colorful Ramakien murals on the walls of the surrounding gallery.

Several notable illustrated manuscripts produced in early Bangkok, most likely inspired by similar ones in Ayutthaya, deal with elephants. These show both the various mythological types from Indian legend and those supposedly found in the natural world. The latter, sometimes shown in forest settings and sometimes standing alone with detailed descriptions, cover a broad range of specimens, from highly desirable ones like the perfect, pure-gold Ubosot to others that should be avoided; according to Henry Ginsburg in *Thai Manuscript Painting,* the worst of all is one called Hinathot, which has a pig-like head, a short tail, and "a horrible great bellow likely to endear it to ghosts and spirits." Other manuscripts of

the same period concern elephant training and their placement in a military formation.

Stylized or realistic, sacred or merely decorative, artistic depictions of the animals can be found in other parts of Bangkok as well. A white elephant is among the 108 auspicious signs rendered in delicate mother-of-pearl inlay on the feet of the huge Reclining Buddha at Wat Phra Chetupon (Wat Po), and Erawan with the monkey-god Hanuman on his back appears on a window panel decorated with scenes from the Ramakien. Multi-colored elephants roam through the mythical Himaphan forest, some of them offering flowers to Buddhist monks, in mural paintings that cover walls at Wat Suthat. The elephant-headed Ganesha is the symbol of the Thai Fine Arts Department, and a statue of him stands outside the National School of Dance and Dramatic Arts. On Phya Thai Road, elephants adorn one of the bridges opened annually by King Chulalongkorn to celebrate his birthday. Erawan forms part of the emblem of the Bangkok Metropoli-

Above top: Ganesha statue in front of the National School of Dance and Dramatic Arts; the elephant-headed son of Siva and Pavarti is particularly revered by artists and students.
Above bottom: Royal seal from the reign of King Chulalongkorn bearing an image of Erawan.

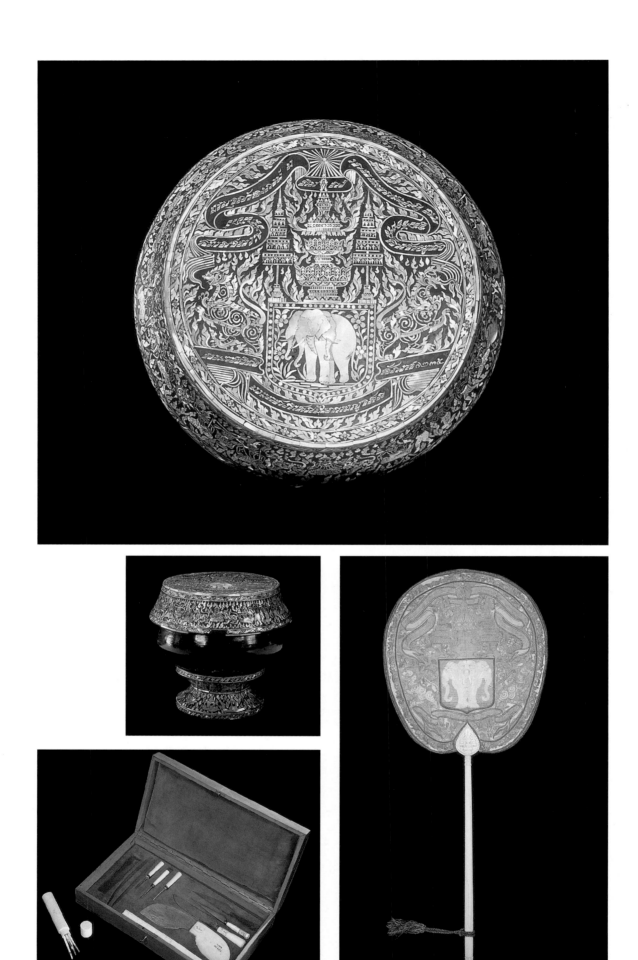

Above: Gifts from King Rama V for the American Centennial Exposition in 1876 include a silk prayer fan with an ivory handle and a mother-of-pearl inlaid lacquer monk's alms bowl, both with images of Erawan, as well as a set of ivory-handled knives and artist's tools. (Courtesy of The Smithsonian Institution)
Following spread: Pages from illustrated manuscripts dealing with elephants.

๏ กชหนึ่งศุภลักษณสาร ใหญ่สูงบวร ชื่อกาละวักหักดี มีพรรณโสภาคยกำคี เหมือน
ปีกกาปี กังรักษธันเหลื่อมเปนมัน มีฤทธิกำลังมหนก หัวหักแฬงาน ธรินทเสี้ยนศักสยม
มียศบริวารมูลมง ภกกมายเนืองนอง มาเวกมกอัมหศคิน กำลังอยกว่านาคินท ถึงสิบ
เท่ากวิล จึงเทียบคังใดยศุภกช   ๚   ๚   ๏

๏ จกสาวธุทิศกำหนก ชื่อไอยภพก พิฬิทธเฟียงเมฆ กายใหญ่เทวิฬุสไสภก เท่าเทียม
บวรพก ศรีกวกังเมฆเทียมทัก ทั่วหน้กลมกลอ่มกลนิกร ทั่วหลังเวียงวัก แลเกินนั้น
เรียบเสมอกัน งอนอรันขวาสวพสรรพ งวงงามเนิดฉัน กังนากกชฤทธี กกังถาวปกายพ์ฤกช
มี แทงบังศลองศี ปลายหูทังสองปรบกัน จกหน้าจรกหลังสำคัญ หลังภาปเรียบวนั กระถมอก
ทังสองสงไขย เสียงวองเสียงเมฆเกรียงไกรย เสียงกุกสังใส สถิกยอยู่บรพทิศก   ๚ ๏

๏ ช้างหนึ่งทายนามสมยา ศุภลักษณโสภา ชื่อเสาวไกรมีพรรณ กายกลมกุจใส่เลื่อน
ศรีเควเขียวขัน กังหญ้าอันอ่อนสกใส มีมุกรมหันกดำไกย ศรีกระแกงไป กามงามแลทัณ
ต่อทาง บริสุทธมานยัยวาวนวง ตาก่ำพิศพงค์ เมื่องัสกัสเสียงนกเรียน กล้าหารบริปัก
สยองเคียร สลิกยศส่เสียร ยังทิศจุกวไกยมี ๚ ๚ ๛

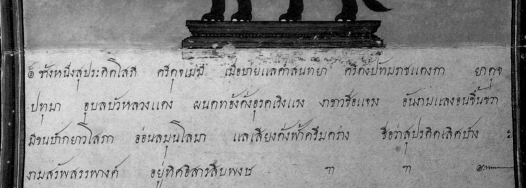

๏ ช้างนึ่งสุประกิกโสกี ศรีกุงเมมี เมื่อบ่ายแลก่ำสนทยา ศรีกังปัทมภาชแกงกา ยากจ
ปทุมา อุบลบัวหลวงแกง ผนกทยังกังอุ๊กเชิงแง งาทาชื่อแฉม อันงามแลงฉนขึ้นขวา
มีขนบักยาวโสภา อ่อนสมุนโลมา แลเสียงกังฟ้าศรีมุกก่ำง ชื่อว่าสุประกิกเลิกบัง ๚
งามสรพสรรพางค์ อยู่ทิศอิสานสืบพงษ ๚ ๚ ๛

Ganesha

Ganesha - also spelled Ganesh and Ganesa, also known by other names such as Vigneshwara, Vinakaya, and Pillayar - is the most omnipresent of the Hindu gods associated with elephants and those who keep them. He is usually represented as having an elephant's head, an enormous stomach, and disproportioned limbs (sometimes four arms), often with his vehicle, a rat, at his feet.

There are several versions of the god's birth. According to one of the most popular, called the *Sivapurana*, Pavarti (Siva's consort) was disturbed by Siva's intrusion during her bathing ritual and miraculously created a glorious being whom she called her son and guardian. When the son tried to stop Siva from entering, the enraged god decapitated him and then, to make amends to Pavarti, promised to attach to the body the head of the first living creature he met - which happened to be an elephant. Another version says it was Pavarti herself who removed the head "by the brilliancy of her look," but agrees that it was Siva who sent out his servants to find a replacement.

In any event, Ganesha became the focus of a complex mythology. He is, one writer says,

"the symbol of the unity of small being, or man - the microcosm - with the great, the elephant - the macrocosm." In one of his aspects, Vigneshwara, he is the "lord of obstacles." The Mahabharata states that he was the scribe of this epic, and thus he became the protector of letters and the god of knowledge. In Hindu Tantrism, symbols representing Ganesha include the yantra (diagram of the swastika) and his attributes include the noose, the elephant goad, his own broken tusk, the disk, and the bowl of sweets.

The cult of Ganesha spread throughout most of Southeast Asia, at first as a member of the Brahmanic pantheon and later in Buddhism. Images have been found in Cambodia from pre-Angkor times, with 7th century figures showing accurate anatomical details of the Asian elephant. In Thailand, he became closly associated with teachers and the arts (he is the guardian of Silpakorn University), with many royal Brahmin ceremonies, and of course, with almost every aspect of elephantry, from capturing the wild animals to their training.

Above: Ganesha statue from the Srivijaya period.
Opposite: Painting of Ganesha on a window panel of Wat Phra Kaew Wang Na, Bangkok.

tan Administration; and an ordinary elephant, seen from the front and holding a traditional garland in its trunk, dominates the insignia of the scholarly Siam Society.

One of the city's greatest elephant concentrations is on view at a shrine next to the Grand Hyatt Erawan Hotel, overlooking a busy intersection. This was erected following a mysterious series of accidents during construction of the government-owned Erawan Hotel in the late 1950s and is actually dedicated to the multi-armed Hindu god Brahma, whose statue is displayed there. Wooden elephants, however, became the most popular offering to the deity, ranging in size from small to huge and presented in such numbers they must occasionally be thinned out to make room for more. (Similar offerings are common and other shrines, especially outside hospitals where, presumably, the wish is for greater strength and longevity.)

The elephant as emblem and artistic inspiration can be found throughout Thailand. It appears, for example, on the official seals of no fewer than seven provinces - Nakhon Nayok (an elephant holding a rice stalk to suggest a fertile land), Suphanburi (the duel on elephant-back between King Naresuan and the Crown Prince of Burma), Chiang Mai (a white elephant in a crystal pavilion), Chiang Rai (a cheerful specimen surrounded by traditional motifs), Tak (King Naresuan again, this time proclaiming Thai independence astride an elephant), Mae Hong Sorn (one swimming in a stream), and Surin (Indra riding on Erawan).

Elephant designs on textiles, often highly stylized, have long been common among the T'ai speaking groups of Southeast Asia, who range from the Assam region of India to Yunnan in China, including parts of northern Burma, Thailand,

Above from top left: The official seals of the provinces of Mae Hong Sorn, Nakhon Nayok, Chiang Rai, Chiang Mai, Suphanburi and Tak. *Opposite:* Shoulder cloth of the T'ai Daeng group in Laos with stylized elephant motif. (Collection of Paothong Thongchua)

182

and Laos. Such mo-  well on *tung*, ban-
tifs are found on *pha* ners or flags hung
chet, or shoulder outside temples on
cloths worn by men, festival days.
woven of white cot-   Contemporary
ton with a supple- Thai artists and
mentary weft design craftsmen continue to
decorating both be just as drawn to
ends. According to the elephant as their
one source, ele- ancestors. On the of-
phants suggested ficial emblem of His

status and thus such cloths were favored by more affluent villagers.

Majesty King Bhumibol's Golden Jubilee in
1996, two white elephants surmounted by

The animal is also seen on textiles
made for religious or ritualistic purposes
- for instance, backdrop cloths for Buddhist altars, a piece to be knelt on in front
of an altar, or one made for wrapping
Buddhist scriptures. Some pieces, not
necessarily displaying an elephant motif, are especially made to serve as head-
pieces and backcloths for the animals
when they take part in various ceremonies such as ordinations. Particularly in
the north and northeast, it appears as

seven-tiered umbrellas flanked the Chakri
seal, and elephant-supported ceremonial
arches - inspired by those erected to welcome
King Chulalongkorn home from a European
trip - towered above Ratchadamnoen Av-
enue. Shops everywhere display them made
of wood, ceramic, nielloware, bronze, silver,
gold, and lacquer. They are fashioned into
chopsticks, cufflinks, and cuddly toys,
printed on tee-shirts, incorporated into
business logos, set as decorative guard-
ians outside the doors of luxury hotels.

Above: Decorations for the Golden Jubilee celebrations in 1996; these were inspired by similar ones *(top)*
erected to welcome King Chulalongkorn home after a trip to Europe in 1908.
Opposite: The elephant is a popular subject for contemporary artists such as Chiang Mai painter
Prasong Thongthawat. (Collection of Bilaibhan Sampatisiri)

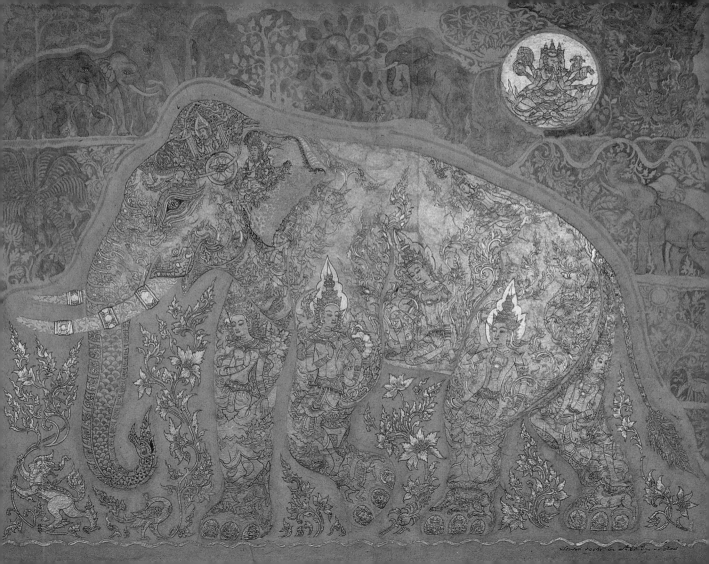

A cushion cover depicting a white elephant has been the biggest seller of all the countless designs offered over the years by the Jim Thompson Thai Silk Company.

In a small community called Baan Chang Nok, outside Chiang Mai, a closely-knit group of skilled carvers has for several decades made a specialty of realistic elephant figures. They use the wood of a local variety of Cassia (*khi lek* in Thai), which is harder than teak, and dip the carvings in a black dye that approximates the color of the animal's skin. Petch Viriya, now perhaps the best-known of the group, learned his skills from another famous sculptor, Kam-ai Dechduanta; his creations, each bearing his initials and a number on the soles of the feet, have been acquired by many eager collectors of elephant art.

A wall of Bangkok's Khao Din Zoo is decorated with fanciful elephants as seen by children, while contemporary painters frequently use the animal to symbolize some aspect of Thai life. Even the howdah is still being produced in elegant forms, though it is more likely today to be seen as an unusual item of interior decoration than bearing notables in a royal procession.

In art and legend, the elephant is still clearly very much a major part of the Thai scene, in no danger of disappearing any time soon. Its prevalence as a cultural icon only underscores the need to help those that remain less visibly in living form.

Above top: A craftsman at Baan Chang Nok outside Chiang Mai. *Above bottom:* Children's art on wall of Khao Din Zoo.
Opposite: The elephant can be seen in all forms throughout the country.

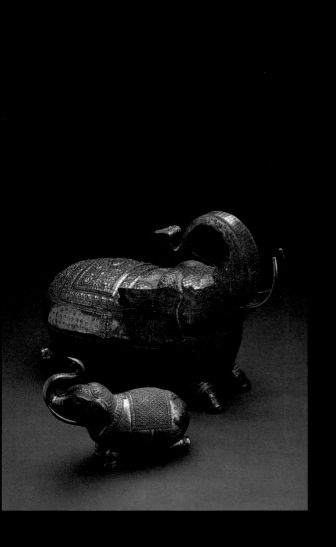

Elephants for Collectors

Elephant lovers often become collectors of elephant art. In cultures where the animal has been an integral part of life and legend, such as those of Thailand, Burma, Laos, and Cambodia, numerous creations fall into this category, both old and new, familiar and unusual. Some are figures made of wood, ceramic, terra cotta, bronze, and precious metals. Others incorporate the elephant into items for everyday or ceremonial use, among them steps used in Buddhist monasteries, candle-holders for altars, coconut graters, pulleys for silk-weaving looms, boxes, devices used for pressing betel-nut and cutting sugar cane, pipes, weights and scales, wrought-iron balustrades, carved panels, and textiles of both silk and cotton.

Such works celebrate not only the elephant but also the skills and imagination of the cultures that produced them.

Preceding spread: Carved spindles from silk looms. The elephant shape is traditional on looms in the northeast. (Courtesy of August 9)
Above top: Silver containers made in Cambodia. *Above bottom:* Bronze elephant made as an offering; height 41 cm.
Opposite: Figure of a walking elephant, made for donation to a temple or shrine; height 58 cm. (All collection of Pratin Hetrakul)

Top row: Carved wooden elephants presented as offerings. *Middle left:* Elephant carving used as step to pulpit. *Middle right:* Bronze elephant, adorned and in devotional attitude.
Bottom left: Papier-mâché elephants, Burmese, used as temple decorations. *Bottom right:* Elephant boxes with riders on the lid. (Collections of Pratin Hetrakul, Neold, August 9, Asian Heritage)

Top: Incense holders in the shape of elephants. (Collections of August 9 and Richard Dixon)
Bottom: Carved wooden candle holders. (Collection of Pratin Hetrakul)

Opposite: Bronze weight, height 22 cm. (Collection of Pratin Hetrakul) *Above top:* Pulleys
from a loom (Courtesy of Neold) *Middle left:* Wooden box, Thai. (Courtesy of Neold)
Middle right: Sandstone elephants, Cambodian; the one on the right is used as a mortar to grind medicine
(Collections of Pratin Hetrakul and August 9) *Bottom:* Wooden coconut grater. (Collection of Pratin Hetrakul)

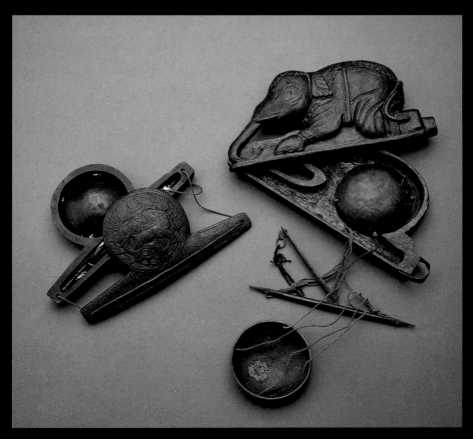

this page from top left: Bronze betel nut masher from Burma, length 11 cm.; wooden pipe, height 4 cm.; earthenware piggy banks from the northeast; scales in wooden boxes. (All courtesy of August 9)

Folk art from northeastern Thailand. *Top:* Wooden box with bone inlay; height 29 cm. (Collection of Prof. Arun Chaiseri)
Above left: Painted boxes with drawers. (Courtesy of August 9)
Above right: Primitive figurines made as offerings for spirit houses. (Collection of Prof. Arun Chaiseri)

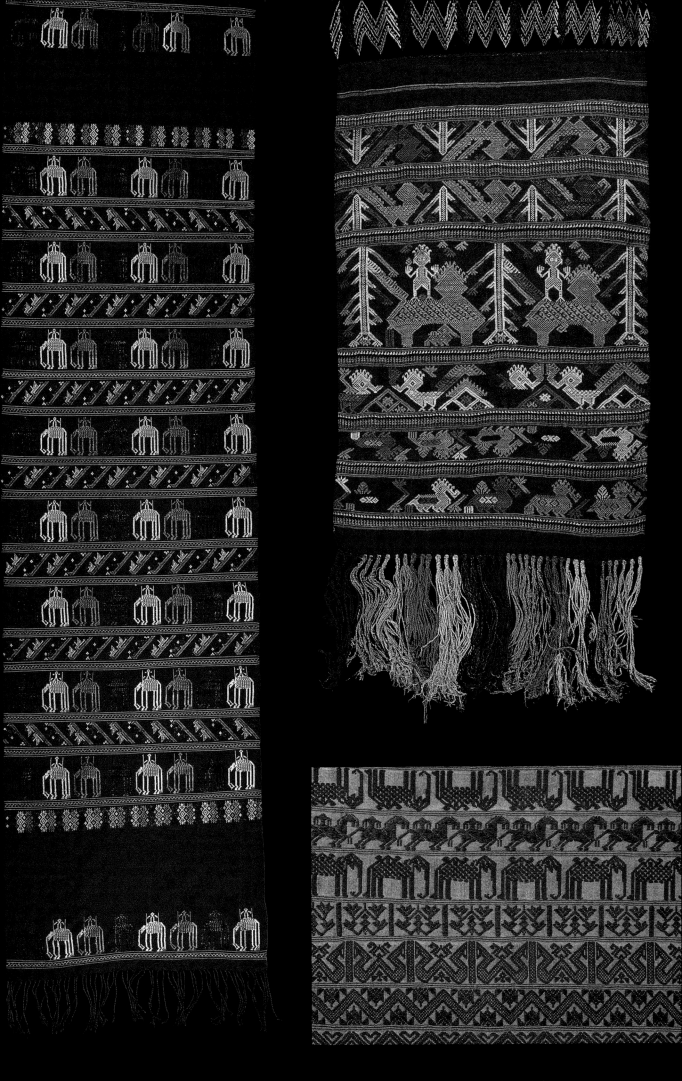

This page: Antique textiles with elephant motifs. *Above left:* Cotton shoulder cloth made in Sakhon Nakorn in the northeast by the Phu T'ai group. *Top right:* Turban belonging to the Sum Nua group in Laos. *Bottom right:* Curtain or altar backdrop from Haad Siew village in Si Satchanalai. (All collection of Paothong Thongchua)

This page: Contemporary textiles. *Top & above right:* Silk *tung* cloth
from Chiang Rai. (Courtesy of The Legend) *Above left:* Cotton sarong from the northeast

Above top: Blanket of the Naga tribe in Burma embroidered with animal figures that include a pair of elephants.
Above bottom: Hand woven cotton textile from Laos. (Both collection of Bilaibhan Sampatisiri)

This page: Elephant head cloth pieces. The elephant is the only animal in Thailand that has a cloth
specifically woven for ceremonial usage. (Collection of Bilaibhan Sampatisiri)

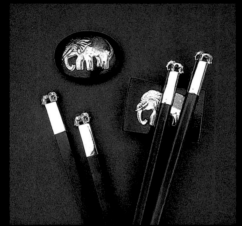

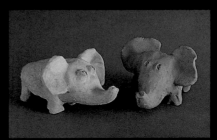

This page from top: Contemporary crafts: neilloware made in Nakorn Sri Thammaraj; shoe horn and paper knives; silver chopsticks & chopstick rests; wooden box; realistic elephant carvings by master craftsmen Nithet Maneekiang and Petch Viriya; ladle with carved handle from Chiang Rai; terra cotta figures by sculptor Nai Dee Changmor. (Courtesy of The Legend, Neold, August 9)

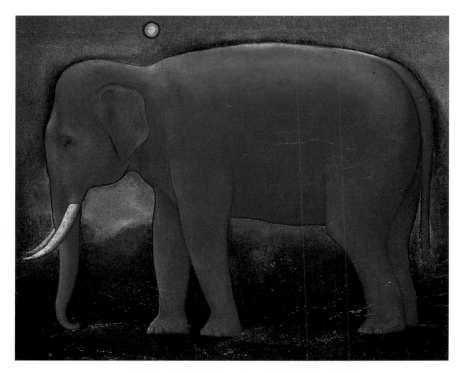

This page top: Ink brush painting by Her Royal Highness Princess Maha Chakri Sirindhorn, who has a special fondness for elephants. (Collection of Bilaibhan Sampatisiri) *Middle:* Painting by contemporary artist Chatchai Puipia. (Courtesy of the artist)
Bottom: Acrylic painting by Sunti Junnongsoung. (Collection of Bilaibhan Sampatisiri)

The Thai Elephant Today

by Richard Lair

In the year 1900 Thailand might have had as many as 100,000 domesticated elephants, and perhaps as many as one man in fifty might have worked at least part time as a mahout, a rider of elephants. An elephant walking through a village would have excited no more attention than a ten-wheel truck does today. The animal played an omnipresent everyday role in art, language, and even religion. Ganesha, the elephant-headed Hindu god, was universally worshipped in Thai temples, while national history was filled with monarchs who had fought and won crucial battles on elephant back - King Ramkhamhaeng, King Naresuan, Queen Suriyothai, and others. Such an ancient cultural presence, coupled with everyday intimacy, explains how the elephant came to be Thailand's unofficial national animal, or *sat khu baan khu meuang khong thai*.

The number of domesticated elephants (sometimes misleadingly called "tame" or "work" elephants) is presently in a steady, inexorable decline. In 1994, according to statistics of the Local Administration Department of the Ministry of Interior, Thailand had about 3,565 domesticated elephants, considerably down from the 5,232 listed by the same agency in 1980. The province with the most elephants is Tak, which had 740 listed in 1994; this is a fact which inevitably surprises Thais, who automatically assume that it must be Surin, home of the world famous Elephant Roundup. (In fact, Surin only has 160 elephants.) The north has about 2,600 elephants, or two-thirds of the national total, although many northern elephants might be recent immigrants, particularly from the northeast but also from the south, which has suffered a precipitous decline to fewer than half of the animals it had in 1980.

Of the eleven Asian countries with domesticated elephants, Thailand is one of the "big three," second only to Burma's approximately 6,400 elephants and slightly ahead of India's 3,000. These three countries collectively hold about 80 percent of the world's total of 17,000 Asian elephants. Compared to other countries, in Thailand the proportion of domestical elephants to wild elephants is very high, about 280 percent. which indicates massive past capture. (Even in elephant-rich Burma domesticated elephants only slightly outnumber wild ones.) Given that over the past thirty years both captures and births have been very few, it must be feared that the average age of many of Thailand's

Previous spread: Elephants and mahouts in Surin.
Opposite: The Karens use elephants for teak logging, transportation and other work, including ploughing rice fields.
Above: A row of elephants at the Thai Elephant Conservation Center in Lampang.

domesticated elephants is far older than that of a natural wild population - and thus that Thailand's high numbers are deceptively reassuring.

Thailand's media have recently showcased a seemingly endless succession of tragedies amongst domestical elephants. In 1993 Honey, a female calf from Surin wandering north and performing for money, was struck by a vehicle in Lamphun, breaking her  pelvis; moved to Bangkok's Dusit Zoo for treatment, she spent three months dying in the media's glare, the first of many cases widely covered by television and the press. In 1995 a young bull named Jockey killed two men tending him and was then himself shot by officials, an act videotaped and later broadcast into millions of homes. In the same year a 23-year-old bull named Phlai Petch became a front-page controversy, even reaching *Time* magazine, because for years he had been constantly kept chained to a tree in a temple. [See sidebar for a fuller account of this case.]

Why have such tragedies become so prominent? Are such horror stories becoming more common or is it simply that the media are now more assiduous in presenting them? The answer is probably a bit of both. The media are now more energetically bringing once obscure stories to the attention of a newly concerned and conservation-

minded public, but today deaths of both men and elephants are undoubtedly more frequent than ever before. The root cause, just as with the crisis facing wild elephants, is development and its inevitable concomitant, deforestation.

Thailand, which was perhaps ninety percent canopy cover at the turn of the century, now has less than fifteen percent natural forest, and most of the valuable timber trees have been logged. The result has been ever decreasing food sources and, even more damaging, ever decreasing work for elephants, a problem that is relentlessly altering elephant-keeping patterns. Traditional owners will not continue to keep elephants unless they can make a living from them.

Historically, probably for all time, the type of work that employed the most elephants was transportation, both of people and goods. Despite its awkward appearance, the elephant is far more adept in mountainous terrain than the horse; elephants also move easily through mud and marshes that will defeat any other animal. At the turn of the century there were said to be 20,000 transport elephants around Chiang Mai and Chiang Rai alone. Warfare employed many elephants, but only a few of the finest were actually trained to combat while probably ten or twenty times more "war elephants" were used solely for transport.

Above: Honey, the injured elephant. *Opposite:* Once a symbol of wealth, elephants today have become almost an economic liability due to a shortage of suitable work.

Phlai Petch: A Case Study

The following, by Richard Lair, is from Gone Astray: The Care and Maintenance of the Asian Elephant in Domesticity, *published by the Food and Agriculture Organization of the United Nations.*

The domesticated elephant's legal status, a non-issue for many decades, in late 1995 suddenly and briefly flared into a contentious public debate in both the Thai and English language press. *The Bangkok Post* of October 16, 1995 headlined: "Cash demand to end elephant's decade in chains." The elephant in question was a 23-year-old bull named Phlai Petch, "Tusker Diamond," which had been kept by itself in a Buddhist temple, nearly always on chains, since he was purchased as a calf of nine months.

Phlai Petch is a walking showcase of a complex of problems newly arisen in modern times: physical and psychological aberrations from premature weaning, malnutrition, poor veterinary care, years in isolation, lack of training, and lack of exercise. His story begs the question of what, in Thailand, constitutes cruelty to animals generally and to elephants in particular, and whether law should be used as an instrument to prevent and punish cruelty. Cruelty is difficult to define anywhere but especially so in Thailand, where a large and vocal urban middle class mostly espouses the same humane values as the contemporary West while in the countryside, given the constant struggle to survive, there is little room for sentimentality towards animals owned primarily to make a living.

The plight of Phlai Petch had worried animal lovers and conservationists for some time. Over the prior year various organizations including the Royal Forestry Department had tried to negotiate with the abbot but he steadfastly refused to part with the animal, as was fully within his rights under the Draught Animal Act of 1939. The situation came to a head when it was noticed that Phlai Petch was being permanently tethered to a tree caught in long-standing flood waters, and that his right foreleg had a wound caused by the tethering chain. At a press conference, Phongsak Vejjajiva announced that the Wild Animal Rescue Foundation wanted to buy the elephant but lacked the 100,000 baht (US$4,000) demanded by the abbot. (The abbot said he needed the money to buy a baby to replace Phlai Petch, a dreadful prospect noted by many observers.) Mr. Vejjajiva "bitterly attacked present animal protection laws and said the elephant is not regarded as a protected animal in Thailand but a draft animal which anyone could obtain and exploit."

The very next day, also on *The Bangkok Post's* front page, the Minister of Agriculture was quoted as saying he "was in favor of a [new] law with penalties for people who restrain wild animals in this way." The minister generously offered to donate 100,000 baht of his own money so that the foundation might buy Phlai Petch, but by that time the essential issue had already been obfuscated. The abbot had, entirely by himself, decided that Phlai Petch was a white elephant and must be given to the King. (Determining whether or not an elephant is truly a white elephant invariably involves many experts for many months.) Even as Phlai Petch's seemingly crystal clear case became ever muddier, his story made *Time* magazine and the nightly television news in the US reported that an elephant was being kept in chains by a "cruel monk." In fact, the beleaguered abbot was genuinely fond of Phlai Petch and could at worst be criticised as misguided or out of step with the times.

What promised to become a rising hurricane of indignation spearheading legal reform thus ended up as a non-story, leaving in abeyance the domesticated elephant's legal status, at least in the public's eyes. Phlai Petch's saga made it clear that the legal questions are a non-story simply because they are too complex to succintly convey in the popular media and too complex for there to be any easy answers. The practical value of Phlai Petch's day in the sun was primarily to provide a public forum for NGOs to raise consciousness, to garner public support, and to greater influence government.

Legally, Phlai Petch's plight made it clear that the Draught Animal Act of 1939's lack of any provisions preventing cruelty made it impossible for the police to invoke the Act to prevent abuse. Article 381 of the Criminal Code could be invoked but its provisions are inappropriate, being intended primarily to prevent cruelty to household pets; in any case, Article 381 is very rarely used by the police. The RFD was totally powerless because the domesticated elephant is specifically excluded from being considered a wild animal by the Wildlife Protection Act of 1992. The legal status of the domesticated elephant in Thailand thus remains in an unhappy limbo, and this is the major importance of Phlai Petch's story.

On December 29, 1996, Phlai Petch managed to free himself from his chains, as he had several times previously, never coming to any harm. He wandered to a nearby community "where his presence caused a commotion." The police were called in, and their sirens and traffic sounds caused Phlai Petch to panic. He "went berserk" and damaged parked vehicles. Ten or more policemen fired a fusillade of over 100 rifle bullets before Phlai Petch fell into a canal and died. Many witnesses said that he was trying to make his way back to the temple.

Opposite: Phlai Phet in musth is screened off by a warning sign and rope. *Below:* Being given a bath as the abbot gives instructions. (Photos courtesy of *The Nation*)

Logging, though it undoubtedly employed far fewer elephants, is far more famous than transportation because it was glamorized in several highly popular books by Teak Wallahs and because dragging heavy logs in harness is intrinsically dramatic, almost gladiatorial. Well-trained elephants can drag logs half their own weight, and being harnessed to such a mass is very dangerous, as can be instantly sensed upon seeing an elephant skid a log down hill or over a rocky river bottom. Many deaths and severe injuries occurred every working season, but at least in the old days the work was seen as sustainable and the elephant as valuable, and thus elephants were largely protected from overwork and abuse.

Unfortunately, since a 1990 ban on logging the only timber work available is skidding illegally-cut logs, a brutal job said by one expert to employ between 1,000 and 1,500 elephants. Illegal logging has forced many conscientious traditional owners to sell and has sent many elephants into the hands of unscrupulous "businessmen" with no love of elephants. Accidents are rife, and there are well-documented cases of elephants being fed amphetamines to make them work harder. Transportation is defunct except for a few trekking tours. Tourism and entertainment now employ perhaps ten percent of the national elephant

population, and one result has been the exhibition of very young calves which are gushed over by people who are unknowing participants in killing the calf by encouraging its owner to separate it from its mother far too early.

The question of unsuitable and dangerous work came to a head when NGOs (non-government organizations) and the public became outraged at elephants being brought into Bangkok to wander the streets selling trinkets and bits of food for passers-by to purchase and feed to the animals. (Virtually all of the elephants came from Surin and all of the mahouts were Kui, or Suay, a tribal people who, ironically, as late as thirty or forty years ago still lasso-captured wild elephants to sell.) Finally, in response to public pressure and bad publicity, the Bangkok Metropolitan Administration banned elephants from entering the city. Unfortunately, the men cannot go back permanently to their home villages, where there is neither income for them nor food for the elephants. The ban has thus not solved the problem but rather moved it elsewhere; instead of confronting the pollution and traffic of a metropolis of 8,000,000 people, more elephants are forced to wander the perilous major highways and the back roads of tourist sites, all of which pose threats different from but no less dangerous than the horrors of the city.

Above: Logging near the Thai-Burmese border.
Opposite: Elephant being transported to the capital to earn money.
Following two spreads: Festival at Ta Klang village in Surin province when boys
to be ordained as monks ride on a procession of elephants.

Thailand presently has between 1,000 and 1,500 wild elephants (about three percent of Asia's population of 38,000 to 48,000), with the largest numbers in two main areas, Khao Yai

National Park and also the Thung Yai and Huai Kha Khaeng Wildlife Sanctuaries. Wild elephants are nearly everywhere threatened by habitat destruction, which constantly eats away at their living space. Poaching occurs, especially of bull elephants being hunted for their tusks, and elephants have just begun to be killed in response to crop raiding. Reports from the border with Burma strongly suggest that sometimes cow elephants are shot solely so that the hunters might capture their calf and sell it. Clearly, this is a wild population in severe trouble.

Two factors ensure that conserving the domesticated elephant is quite different from saving typical indigenous domestic animal breeds such as the many kinds of water buffalo or cattle. First, the Asian elephant has never been selectively bred - man has never systematically over time chosen elephants to mate to create an ideal temperament

or physical type - so the elephant remains both genetically and behaviourally a true wild animal. Second, because most Thai elephants are taken out at night to feed and rest in nature, held only by a tethering chain, perhaps two out of three are pre-conditioned to the wild and would survive if released, either to restock areas where wild elephants have been made extinct, to bolster declining wild numbers, or to correct an imbalance between the sexes. It is as if there were thousands of tigers or Sumatran rhinos or any other endangered species being kept by villagers in anticipation of release, a resource unique in wildlife conservation.

The Asian elephant is an endangered species and thus even elephants in domesticity are fully protected under a treaty called CITES. Conservation and management is more difficult in-country, however, because by law domesticated elephants are private property pure and simple, classified along with cattle, water buffalo, horses, donkeys, and mules under the Draught Animal Act of 1939, a law concerned solely with the rights and obligations of ownership.

Previous spread: Herd of wild elephants in Kuiburi, Prachuap Khiri Khan.
This page top & opposite: Wild elephants in Khao Yai National Park.
This page bottom: Domesticated elephants and water buffaloes come under the same legal category.

The Mahout Today
by Pittaya Homkrailas

Elephant training has been a part of Asian culture for more that 4,000 years. It has also given rise to one of the oldest occupations in the world - that of being a mahout, which according to the dictionary of the Thai Royal Institute means "a person who drives, takes care of, and controls elephants."

Though a mahout no longer enjoys the great prestige of the past, when he captured wild elephants and took part in wars, he must still have exceptional qualities. The most important of these is a thorough knowledge of his animal. He must know how to reward an elephant when it does something right or punish it when it does wrong, and how to communicate by nudging the elephant's ears with his toes, pressing with his legs, rocking himself, shouting, and using a hook or knife at strategic places. He must realize that a blunder may cost him money, since he is expected to pay for any damages caused by his elephant, or even his life, since elephants are potentially dangerous animals.

Most good mahouts are men who have been close to elephants since childhood. Families who keep the animals will pass on to their children such lore as plants that can be used for food or medicine and how to make certain necessary tools; young boys also have an opportunity to work with family elephants, thus preparing them for what is often a lifetime with one particular animal.

In Thailand, the largest number of mahouts are Karen-Thai who come from along the Thai-Burmese frontier. There are about 2,500 to 3,000 mahouts in this group, most of whom earn around 7,000 baht a month by hauling logs. Another group consists of Kui people along the Thai-Cambodian border, who earn an estimated 10,000 baht taking part in elephant shows or selling souvenirs at tourists sites. In controlling their animals, Karen mahouts generally use knives, while the Kui use hooks.

Whether Karen or Kui, basic training starts with a ritual asking for the permission and blessing of the spirits who protect elephants so that the process will be quick and smooth. Thereafter, the first stage involves getting the elephant accustomed to chains and having a rider on its neck, as well as teaching it to obey simple commands. A prod accompanies each command until, after repetition, the animal performs the act after hearing the verbal order without any prodding. In the second stage of training the elephant uses its trunk in pushing logs and its tusks for lifting them; those who take part in tourist shows are taught such things as greeting the audience, kicking a ball, or standing up on two legs.

In controlling his elephant, it is essential that the mahout gets to know his elephant well so that he can fully communicate with it. Methods of punishment vary, depending on the seriousness of the animal's misbehavior. If it pulls a branch from a fruit orchard as it strolls past, for instance, and then disobeys an order not to do so again, the mahout may strike its head with the back of a hook, lightly or hard depending on the degree of resistance by the animal. If the elephant does something very dangerous, like injuring a person, it may receive a hard blow on the head or the base of its trunk with the sharp end of the hook, to instill a fear of repeating the offense.

A mahout and his elephant usually have a long-term relationship that ends only with the mahout's death or when the elephant is sold.

Pittaya Homkrailas is the Assistant to the Secretary and a founding member of the Asian Elephant Foundation of Thailand. He has worked with elephants and the Kui people for a number of years.

Elephants are required to be registered with the Ministry of Interior's Local Administration Department, but the LAD has no expertise or capability in veterinary care. Current registration procedures gather so little information that it is impossible to determine average age, work performed, income produced, health, the nature and amount of international trade, etc. The domesticated elephant is specifically excluded from the Wildlife Protection Act of 1992, which would place it under the jurisdiction of the Royal Forest Department. (Some conservationists believe the RFD is the elephant's logical protector, but it is hard to see how the department could ever provide veterinary care and enforce work regulations for more than 3,000 elephants.) The Department of Livestock Development has massive veterinary resources but no legal obligation to care for elephants.

The only elephants which can be said to belong to the entire nation are the eighty animals owned by the Forest Industry Organization, a state enterprise which runs the Thai Elephant Conservation Center in Lampang. In partnership with an NGO, the Friends of the Asian Elephant, FIO runs an adjoining elephant hospital - the first in the world - which treats severely injured and ill elephants.

The stable, idyllic world of the past has been turned upside down in only fifty years, or just about an elephant's life span. Economically, from being a prime symbol and creator of wealth, many elephants have become almost a liability since it is now very difficult to eke out even a bare living except in illegal or unsuitable work. The traditional price structure has turned topsy-turvy, with calves being amongst the most expensive animals whereas they used to be very cheap because they can do no heavy work. While most elephants have declined greatly in value, a few classes have greatly increased because of their rarity - very young calves, very docile and beautiful tuskers, and good performers. Some of the best logging elephants have probably been sold into Burma and Laos.

The most frightening immediate threat to elephants is undoubtedly a grave and rapid decline in the quality of the mahouts. Many tribal keepers have left the profession and the sons of many mahouts are choosing other kinds of work. Increasingly, being a mahout has become the job of very young men with no prior experience, resulting in the deaths of many men and ultimately many elephants, shot because there is no available mahout with sufficient skills to control them. Thailand's foremost elephant veterinarian, Dr. Preecha Phongkham, believes that about 200 mahouts are killed an-

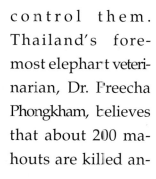

Opposite: Traditionally inexpensive, young calves are now the most highly valued for work in the tourist industry.
Above: Injured elephant at Kasetsart University animal hospital.

nually, with only about fifty deaths being reported to authorities.

The picture is grim. As the most developed of Asia's elephant-keeping nations, Thailand is also the hardest hit by unemployment, poor mahoutship, changing values, etc. As the holder of the second-largest population of such nations, Thailand faces even greater problems than India and Sri Lanka, although they are in very similar circumstances. Since all but a handful of Thailand's nearly 4,000 elephants are privately-owned, providing positive support will surely prove to be very expensive.

Yet there are some bright signs. Thailand's domesticated elephants are lucky to be supported by a few excellent NGOs . Unfortunately, limited by meager resources and manpower, the NGO's efforts, however heroic and important, can make but a small dent in the physical problem - although they do serve an invaluable function in education and in raising public awareness. Several government agencies are also beginning to realize the extent of the problem, and the National Identity Board of the Prime Minister's Office has established a co-ordinating committee.

Conservation is complicated by the fact that the threats facing elephants are incredibly varied, involving not just technical disciplines (such as biology, veterinary medicine, etc.) but also social and cultural disciplines (anthropology, sociology, rural economics, etc.). Clearly, conserving Thailand's domesticated elephants will necessarily involve the entire nation.

Richard Lair has studied and worked with Asian elephants for over twenty years. His book, Gone Astray: The Care and Management of the Asian Elephant in Domesticity, *covers conservation problems across Asia.*

Above: Jum and *Jim,* reportedly the first elephant twins in the world, born in Kanchanaburi, 27th August 1993. *Opposite:* Performance at the annual Surin Elephant Roundup.

The Thai Elephant in Today's Consumer Society

By Pongpisit Viseshakul (Ph.D. Cantab.)

One of the Lord Buddha's most important teachings tells us to lead a moderate life. Yet in today's society, people are turning more and more materialistic, indulging in excessive consumption. This imbalance increasingly affects the well being and existence of wildlife and the ecosystem as a whole. A reflection of this can be seen in the declining number of elephants in Thailand, both wild and domesticated. It is estimated that there are 2,000 elephants in captivity left and only 1,800 to 2,000 in the wild. We can say that elephants are now on the brink of extinction in Thailand.

Consumerism has led to a steady expansion of cities into the surrounding buffer zones. Forests are being encroached by illegal loggers, human settlements and commercial farming. This pushes poor and marginal farmers to degrade the forests further and further without a limit. Forests, once the home and source of food for these wild elephants are stripped bare. Elephants, therefore, need to roam further and in turn, start to 'encroach' and damage villagers' farms which were once forest land. As a result, we regularly read about the often deadly conflicts between elephants and human beings in heartbreaking stories on the front page of newspapers.

The Energy Conservation and Promotion Fund has recently established an information center on energy and natural resources conservation in Pranburi, near Pah La-Ou Waterfall (40 km. east of Hua Hin) where forest areas have been largely exploited and the existence of wild elephants is at risk.

The center's main objective is to promote awareness - among tourists and the public alike - on the impact of excessive consumption on wildlife, plus how to conserve energy and make sustainable use of natural resources. Different kinds of ecotourism, such as trekking in the forest with local villagers acting as tour guides, and observing elephants from towers, will be just some of the activities in this 'natural classroom' to be organized by the center.

The Fund hopes that visitors to this center will come to understand the root cause of conflict between man and elephant and gradually change their wasteful habits. In addition, the success of this ecotourism will generate income for the local people, thus turning elephants into a valuable asset. Ultimately, elephants in the area will be able to co-exist with people, depending on each other, thus maintaining this state of equilibrium and respect between humans and wildlife.

The author is the Director of Energy Conservation and Renewable Energy Division, National Energy Policy Office.

Opposite: Elephants brought by mahout to earn money on the streets of Bangkok. *Below:* The 'natural classroom' at Khang Kachan National Park, 5 km. before entering Pah La-Ou Waterfall, Prachuap Khiri Khan, organized by the Energy Conservation Promotion Fund.

Calendar of Elephant Related Festivals in Thailand

Lampang *Khantok* Banquet
Early February
Held at the Thai Elephant Conservation Center in the Hangchat district of Lampang. Food is presented to elephants in a *Khantok* style (traditional northern banquet).

Salung Luang Procession, Lampang
Early to mid-April
Part of the Songkran celebration in Lampang; a procession around town of people dressed in traditional northern costumes accompanied by elephants and their mahouts and a lot of water splashing.

Elephant Ordination Festival, Si Satchanalai
Mid-April
A tradition of the Tai Puan people: every year prior to the ordination, the boys of Haad Siew village are paraded around town on elephant back dressed in colorful clothing and make-up.

Ta Klang Elephant Ordination, Surin
Similar to the one at Si Satchanalai where elephants are used to parade the monks and novices about to be ordained but even more elephants are involved - as much as 100 in some years. Exact date changes but always before Buddhist Lent, betweeen May and July.

Surin Annual Roundup

Mid-November

The most famous of the elephant related events. Organized by the Tourism Authority of Thailand, the elephant performances include battle re-enactments, elephants playing soccer and elephant roundup demonstrations by the local Kui people.

Flower Blossom Festival

Early December

Takes place in the Tung Kwien forest reserve in the Hangchat district of Lampang. Consists of a parade of elephants in traditional Lanna style.

Ayutthaya Roundup

Mid-December

Takes place at the elephant kraal in the old capital. There is a battle re-enactment and Kui people demonstrate their method of capturing elephants.

■

Preceding spread: Salung Luang procession in Lampang, part of the town's annual Songkran festival in April, which celebrates the traditional Thai New Year.
This spread: Procession of elephants, possibly the largest of its kind, at the annual ordination ceremony in Ta Klang village, Surin province.

Organizations to Help the Thai Elephant

There are several non-government organizations in Thailand helping elephants. Their work varies from running hospitals and mobile units for sick elephants to developing livelihoods for mahouts, seeking improvement in the legal status of elephants and wild elephant conservation. Following is a list of the major ones in alphbetical order.

DOMESTICATED ELEPHANTS:

Asian Elephant Foundation of Thailand
61/4 Soi Pibulwattana 5, Rama VI Rd., Samsaennai, Phayathai, Bangkok 10400
Tel:(66-2)271-4037; Fax: (66-2) 271-4037

Friends of the Asian Elephant
36/15 Moo 2, Ram-Indra Rd. (km.4) Anusawaree, Bangkhen, Bangkok 10220
Tel: (66-2) 521-2758; Fax: (66-2) 552-3824
E-mail: fae@loxinfo.co.th
http://www.elephant.tnet.co.th

THAI's Jumbo Village, Surin
Thai Airways International Public Co. Ltd
98 Vibhavadi Rangsit Rd., Bangkok 10900
Tel: (66-2) 513-0121

Thai Elephant Conservation Center
Km. 25, Hang Chat, Lampang
contact address: Forest Industry Organization, 61 Phaholyothin Rd., Bangkhen, Bangkok 10220
Tel: (66-2) 561-4992, (66-2) 561-4292-6

Treasure Our Elephants Fund
11th Fl., Nai Lert Tower, 2/4 Wireless Rd., Patumwan, Bangkok 10330
Tel: (66-2) 267-8858-9; Fax: (66-2) 267-8860
29/4 Tunghotel Rd., Chiang Mai 50000
Tel: (053) 242291; Fax: (053) 300020

WILD ELEPHANTS:

Seub Nakhasathein Foundation
Kasetsart University Alumni Assoc. Bldg., 50 Phaholyothin Road, Bangkok 10900
Tel: (66-2) 940-5261; Fax: (66-2) 561-2470
E-mail: <seub@internet.ksc.net.th>

Wildlife Fund Thailand
Under Royal Patronage of H.M. the Queen
251/88-90 Phaholyothin Rd., Bangkhen, Bangkok 10220
Tel: (66-2) 521-3435; Fax: (66-2) 552-6083

The Thailand Elephant Art Project

An innovative new way of helping Thailand's domesticated elephants is to turn them into painters. Conceived by two Russian artists, Vitaly Komar and Alex Melamid, this has been successfully employed in zoos throughout North America, with profits from sales going for elephant upkeep.

Komar and Melamid arrived to set up a Thai project in the spring of 1998. In cooperation with an advisory council made up of experts in the fields of wildlife, conservation, and Thai culture, the project will provide occupational retraining for elephants and their mahouts, many of whom are currently jobless. It hopes not only to raise funds through the sale of paintings produced by elephants to tourists, hotels, and galleries worldwide but also to increase global awareness of the plight of Thailand's elephants.

Address: Komar & Melamid Studio, 62 Skillman Ave., #2, Brooklyn, N.Y. 11211
Tel: 718-389-6719
E-mail: elephantart@mindspring.com

Thai Sayings Related to the Elephant

"A white elephant born to the jungle"
Usually applicable to people - such as someone really special who is found in an unlikely environment (for instance, a really good school teacher in a remote village).

"Killing an elephant for his tusks"
Means wasting a huge treasure just to obtain a small item.

"Seeing an elephant as a pig"
Used when someone is not seeing straight or correctly, as when he is overcome by anger or other emotions.

"Tugging an elephant's tail"
Meaning: it's pointless to pull on an elephant's tail when he's determined to go in his chosen direction. Usually applied to a wife who complains of her husband's misbehavior; it's useless to try to pull him back, let him do what he wants and he'll return on his own.

"Covering up a dead elephant with a lotus leaf"
Meaning: When you do something wrong, don't think you can hide it easily; you'll be found out no matter how hard you try.

"Testing your strength against an elephant"
Meaning: don't think you're so strong or clever, it would be like competing against an elephant. Also don't underestimate your opponent.

"Riding an elephant to catch crickets"
Means using a huge, clumsy tool to do a small, delicate job.

"When inspecting an elephant, check it's tail; when inspecting a maiden, check the mother"
Meaning: when looking at something check all aspects. (A good tail was regarded as one of the marks of a desirable elephant in the old days.)

"Once the sugar cane is in the elephant's mouth, it's hard to retrieve it"
Meaning: once something desirable has been given away, you can forget about getting it back; often used to mean when one gives money to corrupt politicians, it's almost impossible to get it back.

"Don't stand in front of the elephant"
Meaning: Don't go looking for trouble, don't be careless.

Photographic Credits

All photographs by Ping Amranand *except:*
The Nation: pages 71, 208, 210, 211, 213, 218-219, 225, 226, 228.
Suthas Roongsirisilp: pages 20, 27, 98-99, 207, 209, 220 (bottom), 224, 227.
Dominic Faulder: pages 100 (bottom), 120, 138, 139 (both), 140, 141.
Kriengkrai Waiyakij: pages 50, 154, 172 (bottom), 184, 204-205.
Sone Simatrang: pages 82, 113, 166, 178, 179.
The Smithsonian Institution: pages 85, 177 (all).

Luca Invernizzi Tettoni (Photobank): pages 10, 37, 72-73, 89.
Bibliothèque Nationale, Paris: pages 8-9, 74-77.
Mark Graham: pages 91 (top), 212, 221, 240.
Saran Boonprasert: pages 58, 100 (top).
Teeraparb Lohitkun: pages 16, 223.
Bureau Bangkok: page 234.
M.L. Prinyakorn Voravan: page 19.
Nakaret Theerakhamsri: page 23.
Nikhom Putra: page 220 (top).
Pattana Decha: page 187 (top right).

Acknowledgements

This book would not have been possible without the generous assistance of many people, to whom the author, photographer and publisher are deeply indebted.

We would like to thank the editorial advisory board chairman, H.E. Anand Panyarachun and all the members of the board: Kusuma Snitwongse Ph.D., M.R. Saisingh Siributr, Dhiravat na Pombejra Ph.D., Ms. Daranee Charoen-Rajapark, Ms. Panitarn Na Pombejra, Mr. Paravee Wongchirachai and Mr. Pana Janviroj.

We owe our gratitude to the sponsors of the project: The National Energy Policy Office, Advance Agro Plc. and Thai Airways International.

For lending us objects and documents to photograph, we are indebted to Professor Arun Chaiseri, Ms. Pratin Hetrakul , Ms. Bilaibhan Sampatisiri, M.R. Supanee Diskul, Mr. Paothong Thongchua, Mr. Robert McCarthy, Mr. Kitisak Hengsadeekul, Mr. Nithi Sthapitanonda, Mr. William Booth and Mr. Eric Booth of the Jim Thompson Thai Silk Company, Mr. Chaiwut Tulyadhan of Neold, Mr. Joerg Kohler of Old Maps and Prints, Mr. Surakit Leeruangsri of 'August 9', Mr. Pornroj Angsanakul of The Legend and Tamnan Mingmuang, Ms. Laurence Dauplay of Asian Heritage, and Mr. Richard Dixon of Siam Gallery in Chiang Mai.

We would like to express our gratitude to the contributing writers : Mr. Richard Lair, Professor Suthilak Ambhanwong, Mr. Pittaya Homkrailas, Mr. Peter Cuasay, Mr. R.W. Wood, and to Dr. Pongsri Lekawatana for supplying excellent translations from Thai sources. We thank the invaluable services of photography assistant/technician Mr. Pattana Decha as well as photographer liason and researchers Saran Boonprasert and Ms. Nipatporn Pengkaew.

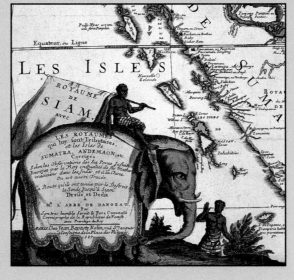

We would also like to thank all contributing photographers: Mr. Suthas Roongsirisilp, Mr. Kriengkrai Waiyakij, Mr. Teeraparb Lohitkun, M.L. Prinyakorn Voravan, Mr. Nakaret Theerakhamsri, Mr. Nikhom Putra and in particular, those who have allowed us to select pictures from their archives namely, The Nation photo library, Mr. Mark Graham, Mr. Luca Invernizzi Tettoni of Photobank and Mr. Dominic Faulder of Bureau Bangkok. In addition, we thank Didier and Marie Claud Millet for providing help in obtaining old documents from the Bibliothèque Nationale in Paris, and Dr. Paul Taylor and Ms. Lisa McQuail of The Smithsonian Institution. We are grateful to the artists who gave us permission to reproduce their work here, namely, Mr. Chatchai Puipia, Mr. Prasong Thongthawat, Mr. Sunti Junnongsoung and Mr. Petch Viriya. Others who have contributed their time and advice to the project include Dr. Pongpisit Viseshakul, Dr. Hakan Kolmodin, Mr. Siddhijai Solasachinda, Ms. Aye Amranand, Mr. Vidhusvasti Amranand, Mr. Thor Santisiri, Asst. Prof. Sone Simatrang, Mr. Athi Chanopas, Ms. Srivara Issara, Ms. Uma Debhakham, Mr. Manit Sriwanichpoom and Ms. Linzy Emery.

And lastly, we thank the following official organizations for their assistance: Office of Her Majesty's Private Secretary, The Royal Household Bureau, the Royal Elephant National Museum, The National Museums in Ayutthaya Chiang Saen and Nan, The Siam Society, the Mae Fah Luang Foundation, The College of Dramatic Arts, The Bureau of Royal Scribe and Royal Decoration, The National Library and The National Archives.

Bibliography

Beauvoir, Marquis de, *A Week in Siam,* January 1867 (The Siam Society, Bangkok 1986)

Bock, Carl, *Temples and Elephants* (reprint by White Orchid Press, Bangkok 1985)

Bowring, Sir John, *The Kingdom and the People of Siam* (reprint by Oxford University Press, Kuala Lumpur, 1969)

Bruce, Helen, *Nine Temples of Bangkok* (Chalermnit Press, Bangkok, 1960)

Carrington, Richard, *Elephants* (The Scientific Book Club, London, 1958)

Choisy, Abbe de, *Journal of a Voyage to Siam 1685-1686* (translation by Michael Smithies, reprint by Oxford University Press, Kuala Lumpur, 1993)

Collis, Maurice, *Siamese White* (Faber and Faber, London, 1936), and The Grand Peregrination (Carcanet Press, Manchester, 1990)

Delort, Robert, *The Life and Lore of the Elephant* (Thames and Hudson, London, 1992)

Dubois, Abbe J.A., *Hindu Manners, Customs and Ceremonies* (Oxford University Press, London, 1906)

Forbin, Claude de, *The Siamese Memoirs of Count Claude de Forbin* (translated by Michael Smithies, Silkworm Books, Chiang Mai, 1997)

Gervaise, Nicholas, *The Natural and Political History of the Kingdom of Siam* (translated by John Villiers, White Lotus Co. Ltd., Bangkok 1989)

Ginsburg, Henry, *Thai Manuscript Painting* (The British Library, London 1989)

Graham, Mark, *Thai Wood* (Finance One Public Company Limited 1996)

Griswold, Alexander B. *King Mongkut of Siam* (The Asia Society, New York, 1961)

Krug, Sonia and Shirley Duboff, *The Kamthieng House: Its History and Collections* (The Siam Society, Bangkok, 1982)

La Loubère, Simon de, *A New Historical Relation of the Kindom of Siam* (reprint by Oxford University Press, Singapore, 1986)

Lair, Richard C., *Gone Astray: The Care and Management of the Asian Elephant in Domesticity* (Bangkok, n.d.)

Leonowens, Anna, *The English Governess at the Siamese Court* (reprint by Oxford University Press, Singapore, 1989)

McQuail, Lisa, *Treasures of Two Nations: Thai Royal Gifts to the United States of America* (Smithsonian Institution, Washington DC, 1997)

Moore, Elizabeth, and Philip Stott, Suriyavudh Sukhasvasti, *Ancient Capitals of Thailand* (River Books, Bangkok 1995)

Na Nagara, Prasert, et. al., *The Inscription of King Ramkamhaeng the Great* (Chulalongkorn University)

Naengnoi Punjabhan and Somchai na Nakhonphanum, *The Art of Thai Wood Carving* (Rerngrom Publishing Company, Bangkok, 1990)

Neale, F.A., *Narrative of a Residence in Siam (1850)* (reprint by White Lotus, Bangkok, n.d.)

Plon-Bernier, Raymond, *Festivals and Ceremonies of Thailand* (translated by Joann Elizabeth Soulier, Assumption Press, Bangkok, 1973)

Reynolds, Bruce and Vimon Bhonghibhat, ed., *The Eagle and the Elephant, 150 Years of Thai-American Relations* (United Production, Bangkok, 1982)

Ringis, Rita, *Elephants of Thailand in Myth, Art, and Reality* (Oxford University Press, Singapore, 1996)

Rong Syamananda, *A History of Thailand* (Chulalongkorn University, Bangkok, 1977)

Sawaddi - 15 Years (Collection of articles published by the American Women's Club of Thailand, Bangkok, 1971)

Segallar, Denis, *More Thai Ways* (Allied Newspapers Ltd., Bangkok, 1982)

Siribhadra, Smitthi, and Elizabeth Moore, *Palaces of the Gods*, (River Books, Bangkok 1994)

Smithies, Michael, ed., *Descriptions of Old Siam* (Oxford University Press, Kuala Lumpur, 1995)

Stratton, carol, and McNair Scott, Miriam, *The Art of Sukhothai* (Oxford University Press, Kuala Lumpur, 1981)

Tachard, Guy, *A Relation of a Voyage to Siam* (reprint by White Orchid Press, Bangkok, 1981)

Tettoni, Luca Invernizzi, *A Guide to Chiang Mai and Northern Thailand* (Pacific Rim Press, Bangkok, 1989)

Thompson, P.A., Siam, *An Account of the Country and the People (1910)* (reprint by White Orchid Press, Bangkok, 1987)

Thai National Team, *Traibhumikatha, The Story of the Three Planes of Existence* (translation for Anthology of ASEAN Literatures, 1987)

U Toke Gale, *Burmese Timber Elephant* (Trade Corporation, Rangoon, n.d.)

Van Beek, Steve, and Tettoni, Luca Invernizzi, *The Arts of Thailand* (Thames and Husdon, London, 1991)

Vella, Walter F., *Chaiyo!* (University Press of Hawaii, Honolulu, 1978)

Warren,William, *The Grand Palace*, (The Office of His Majesty's Principal Private Secretary, Bangkok 1988)

Warren, William, and Tettoni, Luca Invernizzi, *Thai Style*, (Times Editions, Singapore, 1993)

Warren, William, and Tettoni, Luca Invernizzi, *Arts and Crafts of Thailand*, (Thames and Hudson, London 1995)

Wood, W.A.R., *Consul in Paradise* (Souvenir Press, London, 1965)

Wyatt, David K., *Thailand: A Short History* (Yale University Press, New Haven, 1989)

IN THE THAI LANGUAGE:

Ambhanwong, Prof. Suthilak, *Chang Thai* (Matichon Press, Bangkok, 1994)

Chang Ton, (Fine Arts Department and Carlsberg Brewery, Bangkok, 1996)

Eiamkransin, Chalee, *Sayam Duekdumban* (Ton-Or Grammy Company Limited, Bangkok, reprinted 1996)

Limsathaporn, Nathagarn, *Rueng khong Chang* (222 Publishing, reprinted 1994)

Praiwal, H, *Chang* (222 Publishing, reprinted 1994)